# Stepping Stones to Eternity

Jesus from the Quran to the Bible

# Don McCurry

ISBN: 978-1-935843-16-0

Dedicated to the glory of God.

# ACKNOWLEDGMENTS

First of all, I give glory and praise to my Heavenly Father Who chose me to be His child and His servant in working with Christians throughout the world for winning Muslims to Jesus Christ.

To my wife, Mary Jo, who has been my faithful companion, spiritual partner and consistent intercessor for me, brothers and sisters in Christ, and Muslims in all nations.

Special thanks goes out to Kate, my assistant, who month after month proofed, copied and mailed these Stepping Stones as enclosures with our month-end newsletters.

I am deeply grateful for the work of Bryan and Gayle Herde, who have taken these *Stepping Stones*, originally written as monthly compositions, and transformed them into a cohesive set of tools in this book format for Christian workers to use here in the United States and around the world.

Thanks also to Bill Thielker for his creative work in the design and layout of this book. And to Spire Resources for warehousing and distributing all of our books for those wishing to obtain copies.

# TABLE OF CONTENTS

# INTRODUCTION

## Construction and Purpose

Each of us is called to bring our Muslim friend into contact with God's Word, the Bible, so that the Holy Spirit may use it to speak truth with power into the life of the person who reads and hears it. *Stepping Stones* is designed precisely for this purpose.

Originally, each of these *Stepping Stones* was composed once a month over a three-year period. Each of them was intended to stand on its own as a catalyst for drawing Muslims into the Bible to interact with God's Word—that Word which is "living and active; sharper than any double-edged sword, it penetrates even to dividing soul and spirit, joints and marrow; it judges the thoughts and attitudes of the heart" (Hebrews 4:12).

This book has *not* been constructed as a progressive, step-by-step process for using quranic statements about Jesus Christ to win Muslims. Rather, it has been built more as a set of individual tools that have been put together into a single tool box. All the tools have similar qualities insofar as each of the *Stepping Stones* contained in this book utilizes references made about Jesus in the Quran. Each tool in this box, when empowered by the Holy Spirit through prayer and His Word, has the potential to touch the heart of Muslims, drive curiosity, bring conviction, and ultimately, pierce the darkness so that the Light of God may shine brightly into the hearts and minds of our dear Muslim friends. Only the Lord knows which tool, which of these *Stepping Stones*, needs to be used at which point in time.

1

I have chosen to begin with Jesus Christ because He is the most important Truth with which all Muslims—in fact all Christians—must deal. Jesus purposely made Himself the single greatest issue in life with which every individual throughout all time must consider. As the representation of the fullness of the Godhead in bodily form, He established Himself as "the Way, the Truth and the Life," and "no one can come unto the Father but by Me [Jesus]" (John 14:6).

For the sake of organization, I have placed the various *Stepping Stones* into four categories. It is my hope that as you work with Muslims, this dividing of topics will enable you to more readily find what you need when you need it. The categories are:

• Jesus' Stages of Life on Earth

• Jesus' Miracles

• Jesus' Earthly Roles

• Jesus' Eternal Roles

How the Holy Spirit directs in each relationship that you have with a Muslim will vary. The Spirit may guide you to use these *Stepping Stones* in a sequence that is not in the same order as we have placed them in this book. I suggest that you familiarize yourself with all the *Stepping Stones* so that you are prepared to follow the Holy Spirit's leading.

For years I have wrestled with the issue of how to use the Quran in working with Muslims. It has been such a controversial subject among Christian workers. Attitudes range from "It is the devil's book," to some even thinking "It is partly inspired." In this series of chapters, I will not go into a lengthy discussion on all of the varied positions held by a wide spectrum of Christians. But I will put forth my own conclusions, namely, that since the Quran contradicts the Holy Spirit inspired Word of God, our Bible, I do not consider it inspired by God and never use it as such.

In several *Tales That Teach* (McCurry, 2009), men such as Barkat A. Khan, Chaudhry Inayat Ullah Mujahhid, Muhammad Aslam of Pakistan, and Pastor Avtov of Georgia were cited as persons who used the Quran as the starting place for discussions with Muslims. I myself have done the same, as cited in the *Tale* recounting what happened at the mosque in Regent's Park, London, with Suleiman (p. 349).

From years of study, I have learned that the Quran contains hundreds of allusions to biblical characters or thoughts, but always the references are distorted, truncated and, in some cases, devilishly misconstrued. In the early years of ministry, discovering these manglings of Bible stories, characters and doctrines led to anger, disgust and a refusal to have anything to do with the Quran.

But because the Quran is part of the warp and woof of the Muslim mindset, even among illiterate people who get it preached to them from the mosques, it gradually dawned on me that instead of rejecting this book out of hand, it could be used as a starting point for bringing our Muslim friends to want to read the original material in the "Ancient Books," meaning, the Bible, for themselves. In the case of illiterates, to have it read to them.

Finally, it struck me that these quranic allusions, re-tellings, and erroneously quoted citations of biblical material could be used as *stepping stones* to walk the Muslim from where he or she is into the glorious light of God's inspired Word. Hence, the title of this new series, *Stepping Stones To Eternity.*

## Context and Foundations

This is the day of a vast Muslim resurgence. With the passing of Western colonialism and the loss of its grip on Muslim lands, Muslims are now recovering their identity. They are going back to their roots and figuring out who they really are. As they do so, the original spirit of Muhammad, the founder of Islam, is influencing those who now read his book, the Quran.

We can no longer ignore Muslims or their book. It is becoming a "must read" for all who would seek to understand what in the world is going on in our day. Pick up any newspaper, major news magazine or check the news on the internet, and you will read that Muslims figure prominently in the major daily crises of our world.

The problem, then, for us, who are non-Muslims, is how do we relate to these people? If they were small in number the problem would not be so acute. But they are one billion and five hundred million souls (as of this printing, 2011) and multiplying faster than any other block of people. We can no longer ignore them. The question is: How can we, as Christians, relate to them?

*Stepping Stones To Eternity* is written to inform you a bit about the abundant biblical material in the Quran and to suggest ways that you can relate to your Muslim neighbors, starting where they are and introducing them to the sources of the material to which they have not been exposed that has been embedded in what they consider to be their holy book, the Quran.

In the studies to follow, we will take up the significant material in the Quran on Jesus. Then we will describe the quranic treatment of this material and suggest ways for you to bring your Muslim friend to consider the ancient sources of these references and the implication of the new insights they will gain from reading the original, inspired Word.

## Integrity of the Bible and Quranic Confirmation

Throughout the Muslim world you will hear almost everywhere the charge that our Bible has been changed or corrupted. Interestingly enough, the Quran universally states that it came to confirm the previous Scriptures, such as:

2:89, "[T]here comes to them a Book from Allah confirming what is with them..." (Spoken to followers of Moses and Jesus.)

2:97, "[H]e [Gabriel] brings down the (revelation) to thy heart by Allah's will, a confirmation of what went before..."

2:101, "[T]here came to them a Messenger from Allah, confirming what was with them." (Jews and Christians)

2:136, "We believe in Allah, and the revelation given to us, and to Abraham, Ismail, Isaac, Jacob, and the Tribes, and that given to Moses and Jesus, and that given to (all) Prophets..." (This is repeated in 3:84.)

3:3, "It is He [Allah] who sent down to thee (step by step) in truth, the Book, confirming what went before it." (The Torah and the Gospel)

3:81, "[T]hen comes to you a Messenger, confirming what is with you..." (This was spoken to "the People of the Book," that is, Jews and Christians.)

3:93, "Bring ye the Torah and study it, if ye be men of truth." (Spoken to the Jews of Medina. Muhammad

5

thought it was divinely inspired Scripture.)

4:47, "O ye People of the Book [Jews and Christians]. Believe in what we have (now) revealed, confirming what was (already) with you..."

5:47, "Let the People of the Gospel judge by what Allah hath revealed therein."

5:48, "To thee We sent the Scripture in truth, confirming the Scripture that came before it, and guarding it in safety."

5:66, "If only they [Jews and Christians] had stood fast by the Torah and the Gospel, and all the Revelation that was sent to them from their Lord..."

5:68, "O People of the Book [Jews and Christians]. Ye have no ground to stand upon unless ye stand fast by the Torah, the Gospel, and all the Revelation that has come to you from your Lord."

10:37, "The Quran...is a confirmation of (revelations) that went before it..."

10:64, "No change can there be in the Words of Allah."

10:94, "If thou wert in doubt as to what We have revealed unto thee, then ask those who have been reading the Book [previous Scriptures] before thee."

46:12, "And before this, was the Book of Moses as a guide and a mercy: and this Book confirms (it) in the Arabic tongue."

57:27, "We sent after them [the previous prophets] Jesus the son of Mary, and bestowed on him the Gospel."

All of these references add up to a tremendous confirmation of the Bible. They name the Torah and the Gospel. They state that there can be no change in the Word of God. The Quran confirms all previous revelation, including what was given to all the Prophets. This is an awesome affirmation of the authenticity of our Scriptures. And we need to remind our Muslim friends over and over again of this.

## The Historical and Legal Defense of Scripture

In spite of the all the quranic confirmation of the Bible listed above, one is apt to meet Muslim friends who still claim that the Bible has been changed or corrupted. Following are several points to use in answering these false charges:

- There are approximately 4,000 ancient documents, all of which pre-date Muhammad, which confirm the text of the Bible as we have it today.

- These manuscripts are on display in various museums around the world and can be viewed by the public.

- The Dead Sea Scrolls, with much of the Old Testament written on them, have been dated about 100 B.C., which is a hundred years before Christ. They were written in the Hebrew Language. When they were compared with the modern Hebrew text of the Old Testament (Torah, Psalms and Prophets), there was virtually no change in the text over the last 2,100 years.

- Before the age of printing, typewriters and computers, all these ancient documents were copied from one generation to the next by hand. Once in a while, a copyist would make a mistake in copying, like forgetting a dot or adding a digit to a number. These are copyist errors. None of them has changed any of the meaning of the

7

original text. It does not mean the original text was changed.

- There is no evidence from any period of history, after the text of the Bible was established, that indicates the Bible is any different today than it was after the text was established hundreds of years before Muhammad.

- Finally, there is the legal approach: If people are going to make accusations that the Bible has been changed, then they have to do the following:

  - They have to show that they have access to the original.

  - They have to prove who changed it.

  - They have to prove when the change took place.

  - They have to show what the changes are compared to the original which they claim to have in their possession.

No one has ever been able to do this. The reason is that there have been no changes and the Bible is not corrupted.

All of the above, including the quranic affirmations of the Bible, and the lack of any historical proof of the corruption of the Bible means that we may use it with integrity with our Muslim friends when we lead them from quranic references to Jesus. The rich and fuller accounts in the Gospel throw more light on His great life and ministry.

Long before Muhammad's time (570 to 632 A.D.), the text of the Old and New Testaments was firmly established for all time. So when people translate the Bible from the original Hebrew, Aramaic and Greek languages into other languages, they are all working from the same standard text.

But very often translators have many choices of words to use in the translation. Not all translators make the same word choices. This is why various translations may not all look alike. But this does not mean that anyone changed the original text of the Bible. No, the original has not been corrupted.

Similarly, for our Muslim friends who can read English, please note that we now have 81 different translations of the Quran in the English language. I am sure that the Muslim scholars all worked from the same standard text of the Quran. The existence of various translations does not mean that anyone corrupted the original.

For those of you interested in Pakistan, it may be of interest to note that there are now more than 300 translations of the Quran in the Urdu language. Again, this does not mean that the original is corrupted.

## Jesus in the Quran

"The Quran gives a greater number of honorable titles to Jesus than to any other figure of the past. Three chapters or *suras* of the Quran are named after references to Jesus (3, 5 and 19); He is mentioned in fifteen *suras* and ninety-three verses. Jesus is always spoken of in the Quran with reverence" (Parrinder 2003:16).

In *Sufi* Islam (Islamic mysticism), Jesus is a constant theme. Sufism, by the way, has permeated all branches of Islam, affecting fifty percent of all Muslims worldwide. In *Jesus in the Eyes of the Sufis*, Dr. Javad Nurbakhsh has forty chapters on different themes of Jesus in Sufi poetry. In his bibliography he lists fifty-seven books on this subject!

A further quote to heighten your interest in sharing your knowledge of Jesus with your Muslim friend comes from Stephen Schwartz' *The Other Islam: Sufism and the Road to Global Harmony*: "[T]he main notable aspect of *Sufism* is its reconciliation of Islam and Christianity through the identification of Jesus, named *Isa* in Islam, as a messenger of divine love."

Islam and Christianity cannot be reconciled, but the Sufi effort to do so demonstrates the problem that Islam (orthodox and mystical) has with what to do with Jesus.

In the Quran, Jesus' name is linguistically altered and takes the form of *Isa*. This is a tragedy because in Arabic the word *Isa* has no meaning. In Hebrew, Jesus' name is *Yeshua* (Joshua in English), meaning "The Lord saves." In Greek, "Jesus" is brought over as *Aysous*, and in Matthew 1:21, we read that He will save His people from their sins. Furthermore, in Matthew 1:23, He is given the name Emmanuel, meaning "God with us." Putting these two ideas together, we have then the concept of "God our Savior is with us."

*Isa* in the Quran is a newly minted word in the Arabic language and perceived simply as a title, but without carrying any meaning. When Muhammad wanted to build his religion, Islam, on the foundation of the Jewish and Christian scriptures (which he only knew by hearsay), he did so with no background in either the Hebrew or Greek language. So he brought over Jesus' name into the Quran as a word with no etymological history and streamlined into the word "*Isa*." This means that the Muslim, reading this word in the Quran, will not have a clue as to what Jesus' name really means, nor what His real ministry was to be.

Dear friend, you can look at this travesty either as a

clever ploy on the part of the Adversary to keep millions of Muslims in the dark and walk away in disgust, or you can look at this as God's opportunity to sit down and patiently work with your Muslim friend to explain who Jesus really is. Please choose to engage with your Muslim friend.

In doing so, remember there are verses in the Quran that give you grounds for bringing understanding to your Muslim friend. In Quran 10:94, we read, "If you [Muslims] are in doubt concerning what We [God] revealed to you, ask those who read the book [the Bible] before you" (Khalidi translation 2008:169).

## Key Words and Terms

There are a few Arabic words and terms which are used repeatedly throughout these *Stepping Stones*, so it seems best to explain them at this point rather than continually repeating myself throughout each chapter. Some of the commonly used terms are:

*Hadith* = Books of Traditions: the written traditions of Islam, based upon Sunnah ("The trodden path," the living tradition concerning what Muhammad did and said).

*Injil* = Gospel or "good news."

*Isa* = Jesus (*Isa* has no meaning in and of itself, unlike Jesus or Joshua, as discussed earlier).

People of the Book = a frequently-used quranic term referring to Jews and Christians.

*Sura(h)* = a chapter or division of the Quran, carrying a number and a title.

## Getting Started

Now it is your turn to bring your Muslim friend to "the Book" [the Bible] and show what *Isa* really means. Matthew 1:21 reads, "She [Mary or *Miriam* in Arabic] will give birth to a son, and you are to give Him the name Jesus [*Joshua* in Hebrew, meaning "the Lord saves"], because He will save His people from their sins."

May the Lord lead you to Muslims and give you the courage to share the true Scriptures with them, which will open their eyes and bring them out of their darkness into God's light.

# JESUS' STAGES
# OF LIFE
# ON EARTH

# THE VIRGIN BIRTH IN QURAN AND BIBLE

Our Muslim friends are the victims of misinformation about what we Christians actually believe. Every Muslim I have ever talked to believes we worship three Gods: Allah, Mary and Jesus.

We can see how this misunderstanding arose in the mind of Muhammad (d. 632) because of his environment. He heard such expressions as "Mary, the Queen of Heaven." Obviously, this implied that she was married to "the King of Heaven." And it follows that their son, sexually begotten, would be called "the Son of God." Added to this was the reference he heard to the "Holy Family," which he took to mean God, Mary and Jesus. The situation was further confused when Muhammad heard Mary being addressed as "the Mother of God," rather than the mother of Jesus.

It is most unfortunate that all of these ideas were given expression in Muhammad's presence. They, of course, were abhorrent to him, especially the idea that God had sex with Mary. Muhammad was a strict monotheist, believing in one God who had no partners, that is, God had no wife (Q. 6:101, "How can He have a son when He hath no consort [wife]?"). With this kind of background information, it is understandable that every time Muhammad heard the expression, "Son of God," he assumed it meant that the speaker thought God had sex with Mary. He rightfully labeled this as a blasphemy.

What is surprising is that the Quran actually upholds the idea of Jesus being miraculously born of the Virgin

Mary. Let's have a look at the quranic rendition of this. There are two passages that speak of Jesus' birth: Q. 19:16-29 and Q. 3:42-47, the latter being the one we will work with here. In this passage, we note that an angel appeared to Mary and said, "O Mary, Allah [God] giveth thee glad tidings of a Word from Him: his name will be Christ Jesus, the son of Mary, held in honor in this world and the hereafter and of those nearest to Allah "(verse 45). In verse 47, we read of Mary's response: "O my Lord, how shall I have a son when no man hath touched me?" "He [the angel] said: 'Even so, Allah createth what He willeth: When He hath decreed a matter, He but saith to it, "Be" and it is!'" This, and the passage in Q. 19, is all the Muslim has to go on with regard to the virgin birth of Jesus.

In whatever way the Lord leads, you should take up the issue of your Muslim friend's misunderstanding and suggest that the original story as found in the Gospel has many interesting details which are worth reviewing.

At this point, open your Bible to Luke 1:26-38, and preferably, have your friend read the passage for himself or herself. The following new ideas will be surprising to them:

- The angel Gabriel visits Mary in the town of Nazareth in Galilee.

- Joseph is named as her betrothed and he is descended from David.

- The angel told Mary she was going to become pregnant without "knowing" a man and that she would have a son named Jesus. Explain that "Jesus" is a name with a meaning, that is, Deliverer or Savior. You may want to use Matthew 1:21 here which explains that Jesus will save His people from their sins.

- Jesus will be called "The Son of the Most High," and He will be given a kingdom that will never end (Luke 1:32-33)—an eternal kingdom associated with David and Jacob.

- When Mary protests that she is a virgin and doesn't understand, the angel explains that the Holy Spirit will overshadow her (no sex here) and that the holy one to be born will be called "the Son of God."

- Mary accepts her role, and while visiting her relative Elizabeth, Zechariah's wife, she breaks into song, praising the Lord for remembering His promise to Abraham (Luke 1:46-55).

As is always the case, the Quran, in referring to this event of old, leaves out so many of the significant details, the most important of which are that Jesus will be a Savior, He will inherit an eternal kingdom, He is the climax of God's promises to Abraham, Jacob/Israel, and David, and that He will be called "the Son of God," "the Son of the Most High."

Since Jesus is called "The Son of God," in the context of the virgin birth, there is not the slightest possibility of hinting that there is any sexual relationship between God and Mary.

If your Muslim friend falls back on the baseless charge that the Christians have changed the Scripture, you may have to use his own book, the Quran, to remind him that there can be no change in the Word of God (Q. 6:34, "[T]here is none that can alter the Words of Allah," and Q. 10:64, "No change can there be in the Words of Allah.").

Love your Muslim friend. Be patient. Be persuasive. Be in prayer.

# JESUS AND THE HOLY SPIRIT

What does the Quran have to say about the Holy Spirit? The answer? Not much. Interesting, isn't it? The New Testament is loaded with references to the Holy Spirit. Look at some of these verses. Jesus and the apostle Paul said:

- "[N]o one can enter the kingdom of God unless he is born of water and the Spirit." John 3:5

- "[T]he Holy Spirit, whom the Father will send in my name, will teach you all things and will remind you of everything I have said to you." John 14:26

- "[T]he Spirit of truth ... will guide you into all truth." John 16:13

- "But you shall receive power after the Holy Spirit comes on you." Acts 1:8

- "[T]he Spirit of life set me free from the law of sin and death." Romans 8:2

- "[T]he mind controlled by the Spirit is life and peace." Romans 8:6

- "[T]hose who are led by the Spirit of God are sons of God." Romans 8:14

- "[T]he letter [law] kills, but the Spirit gives life." 2 Corinthians 3:6

- "[T]he fruit of the Spirit is love, joy, peace..." Galatians 5:22

19

One would think that for all of his exposure to Christians living in Arabia in his lifetime, Muhammad (570-632 A.D.) would have picked up a great deal about the Holy Spirit. That is not the case.

There are only five references in the Quran to the Holy Spirit. In two of them, the Spirit is associated with angels (Q. 70:4, 78:38). In a third, the Spirit is mentioned in connection with inspiration, but then is interpreted to be the angel Gabriel, who supposedly brought the Quran to Muhammad (17:85).

It is the remaining two references that fascinate us and really open wide the door to share powerful material with your Muslim friend.

In Quran 2:87, and 2:253, we read, "We [God] strengthened him [Jesus] with the holy spirit." That is the best you are going to get from the Quran. The question is, what can we do with this statement? Much.

Stop and think for a moment. What happened at Jesus' baptism? "As soon as Jesus was baptized, He went up out of the water. At that moment heaven was opened, and He saw the Spirit of God descending like a dove and lighting on Him. And a voice from heaven said, 'This is my Son, whom I love; with Him I am well pleased'" (Matt. 3:16-17).

What a shock this is for a Muslim! There are ideas here that go completely counter to what they have been taught. Let's take the ideas up, one by one.

First of all, there is not even a whisper in the Quran or the Books of Traditions (the *Hadith*) that God is our Father. No Muslim has ever called God "Father." And here in this passage the voice from heaven is calling Jesus His Son.

Only a father would do that. When Jesus taught His disciples to pray, He began, "Our Father in heaven, hallowed be Your name" (Matt. 6:9). It is your privilege to explain that God is our Father and He intends for us to be His sons and daughters (2 Cor. 6:17-18).

The second shock for a Muslim is that God would open heaven and speak down to earth and put His approval on the beloved Son whom He sent as His representative. Your Muslim friend may have a knee-jerk reaction to this and fall into the mindset whereby he would ask, "How could God have a son when He doesn't have a wife?" Remind your friend that even the Quran testifies to the Virgin Birth of Jesus (Quran 3:47). God only has to speak and it is done.

The third area that will be such a surprise to your friend is that he or she has no real knowledge about the Holy Spirit. Sadly, some Muslim commentators have actually said the Holy Spirit is the angel Gabriel. There is no idea that the Holy Spirit of God is eternal. Nor is there any idea that we were designed to be temples of the Holy Spirit (1 Cor. 3:16), or that we have to be born again by the Spirit (John 3:5), or that we have been sealed by the Holy Spirit (Ephesians 1:13; 4:30).

From the Scriptures you should be able to point out that Jesus did not begin his ministry until the Holy Spirit came upon Him, and that it is only by the Spirit of God that He could cast out demons (Matt. 12:28) and heal people (Acts 10:38). You may want to add that even today, God gives His Spirit and works miracles among those who believe (Galatians 3:5), and that the gift of the Spirit is the final fulfillment of God's promise to Abraham (Gal. 3:14).

Finally, and hopefully, your friend will want to

know how to receive the Holy Spirit. A good place to find the answer is in Peter's sermon on the day of Pentecost. In Acts 2:38, we read, "'Repent and be baptized, every one of you in the name of Jesus Christ for the forgiveness of sins. And you will receive the gift of the Holy Spirit.'" You may have to do a lot of explaining here. So be ready.

My dear Christian friend, I hope I have not lost you. I am trying to give you hope in place of despair. Muslims can be won to the Lord through any believer who is willing to learn the Word of God well enough to be able to use it, and who is willing to start where the Muslim is with his or her Quran. It has all of these references to Jesus and the Holy Spirit, but they have no understanding of what in the world was being referred to by Muhammad.

Please ponder these things and begin to pray that God will give you a Muslim friend with whom you may begin to share these thoughts. Above all, don't be afraid, "Perfect love drives out fear" (1 John 4:18).

# JESUS' DEATH

*So peace is on me the day I was born, the day that I die,*
*And the day that I shall be raised up to life.*[1]
Quran 19:33

*For what I [the Apostle Paul] received I passed on to you as of*
*first importance: that Christ died for our sins according to the*
*Scriptures, that He was buried, that He was raised on the*
*third day according to the Scriptures....*
1 Corinthians 15: 3, 4

It is obvious from the quranic quote above that Muhammad was familiar with the events surrounding Jesus' birth, death and resurrection. Just recall from the Scriptures these words:

- At His birth: "Glory to God in the highest, and on earth peace to men on whom His favor rests" (Luke 2:14).

- On the eve of His death: "Peace I leave with you; My peace I give you. I do not give to you as the world gives. Do not let your hearts be troubled and do not be afraid" (John 14:27).

- At His resurrection: "On the evening of that first day of the week, when the disciples were together, with the doors locked for fear of the Jews, Jesus came and stood among them and said, 'Peace be with you.'

---

[1] Supposedly, Jesus is speaking as a child from his cradle.

Again Jesus said, 'Peace be with you! ...'" (John 20:19, 21).

Characteristically, Muhammad recasts the biblical account in his unique epigrammatic way, leaving out the rich details the Bible records. Kindly invite your Muslim friend to look at these biblical references with you. If possible, read as much of the surrounding verses needed to get the flow of the narrative. In the above quranic passage, there is no doubt that Muhammad was using these words in the identical way in which he applied them to John the Baptist. Supposedly God is speaking: "So peace on him [John the Baptist] the day he was born, the day that he dies, and the day he will be raised up to life" (Quran 19:15).

Since Muslim commentators acknowledge that John the Baptist was killed by King Herod during Jesus' lifetime, the identical thoughts (supposedly) expressed by Jesus in Quran 19:33, indicate, according to the Quran, that Jesus was predicting His death in His own lifetime— not in some far-off, indefinite date in the future. Keep this in mind as you now move to a very problematic passage concerning Jesus' crucifixion, as spoken of by Muhammad: "They [the Jews] said in boast, 'We killed Christ Jesus the son of Mary, the Messenger of Allah;'" But they [the Jews] killed him not, nor crucified him...for of a surety they killed him not" (Quran 4:157).

In the above passage, according to its context, Muhammad is in a furious debate with the Jews of his city. And he is refuting their claims that they, the Jews, killed Jesus.

This leaves the door open for the real facts concerning the death of Jesus. It was the Roman governor Pontius

Pilate who gave the order for Jesus' crucifixion, and it was the Roman soldiers who carried out his orders. The Scripture even says that a Roman soldier thrust a spear in Jesus' side as He hung dead on the cross (John 19: 34).

But there are two other important truths to present to your Muslim friend:

1. Both Peter and Stephen attest to the guilt of the Jews for putting Jesus' to death (Acts 2:36 and 7:52); and

2. Jesus' voluntarily gave His life for all people—no one took it from Him (John 10:17, 18).

Because of the Christian heresies abounding in Arabia at the time of Muhammad (570-632 A.D.), there were many theories as to whether Jesus really died or not. Some said it just *appeared* so. This is reflected in the same quranic verse quoted above (4:157): "And those who differ therein [about the death of Jesus] are full of doubts, with no (certain) knowledge, but only conjecture to follow..."

It is at this point that you, the Christian, should invite your Muslim friend to read with you one of the gospel narratives concerning the arrest, torture, trial and death of Jesus. Of course, the story would not be complete without the subsequent account of the resurrection of Jesus and His ascension into heaven. The Gospel of John, chapters 18 through 21, would be a good place to start.

As you work with your Muslim friend in the biblical Scriptures, be patient and persevering. If objections are raised that the biblical account is not true and that the Bible has been corrupted, please gently take your friend back to the material on the claims of the Quran to confirm the previous Scriptures and recommendation to consult the earlier Scriptures (Q. 6:34, 10:37, 10:94). Also point out that there is no evidence in history that would indicate Jews or Christians did any such thing as change the Scripture.

Remember that for fourteen hundred years, it has been the common Muslim understanding that Jesus did not die on the cross but that God took Him alive to heaven. Only the living and true God can break through this entrenched barrier of misunderstanding drilled into the minds of Muslims for these many long centuries.

But He is able. Nothing is impossible with Him. In every way possible, use His Word, for

*"Is not my word like fire,"* declares the Lord, *"and like a hammer that breaks a rock in pieces?"*
Jeremiah 23:29

# JESUS' SACRIFICE

*[Abraham says] "O my son!*
*I have seen in a dream that I offer thee as a sacrifice..."*
*[The son] said: "O my father, do as thou art commanded:*
*Thou will find me, if Allah so wills, one of the steadfast."*
Quran 37:102

*"I swear by Myself," declares the Lord, "that because you*
*[Abraham] have done this, and have not withheld your son*
*[Isaac], your only son, I will surely bless you...and through*
*your offspring all nations on earth will be blessed,*
*because you have obeyed Me."*
Genesis 22:16-18

These two passages are well worth studying: the quranic (Q. 37:100-113) and the biblical (Gen. 22:1-18). Interestingly, the quranic passage does not mention the son by name. But since around the twelfth century, Muslims have injected the name of Ishmael into this account. It seems that Muslims, aware of the typology of Abraham's son, Isaac, pointing forward to Jesus, who was also called in Scripture "the son of Abraham" (Matt. 1:1), have in these later centuries tried to Islamicize the story in their favor.

Be that as it may, the historical event is about Isaac, through whom the Messiah came, not through Ishmael. When it is appropriate, engage your Muslim friend in a look at the biblical account. Point out that all nations could not be directly blessed through Isaac, who has passed on to glory, but it must be through his more famous descendant,

Jesus, that the nations are being blessed. All Muslims concede that Jesus is alive in heaven today.

If your Muslim friend is willing to continue with you, you may want to go to New Testament material which states that Jesus is Abraham's seed (Gal. 3:16), "The promises were spoken to Abraham and to his seed. The Scripture does not say, 'and to seeds,' meaning many people, but 'and to your seed,' meaning one person, who is Christ."

Beyond this explanation, we find even more material which comments on the nature of Abraham's faith that is germane to our discussion about Isaac being a "type" of Christ. Look at Hebrews 11:17-19:

> By faith Abraham, when God tested him, offered Isaac as a sacrifice. He who had received the promises [to bless the nations] was about to sacrifice his one and only son[1], even though God had said to him, "It is through Isaac that your offspring will be reckoned." Abraham reasoned that God could raise the dead, and figuratively speaking, he did receive Isaac back from death.

This comment from the New Testament scriptures then strengthens the analogy that Isaac was a pre-figuration of Christ, Abraham's seed, who was raised from the dead.

Muslims, as you surely know by now, claim that Jesus was taken alive from the cross and therefore did not die and hence did not rise from the dead.

The Apostle Paul, using the term "gospel" (meaning "good news," *Injil* in Arabic), defines "good news" as follows

---

[1] In the Bible, Ishmael was considered a slave child, and not Abraham's legal son. See Genesis 21:12 for this reference.

(1 Cor. 15:3b-4): "Christ died for our sins according to the Scriptures; He was buried, He was raised on the third day..."

In the same chapter, Paul goes on to explain in 1 Cor. 15:21, 22, "For since death came through a man, the resurrection of the dead comes also through a man. For as in Adam all die, so in Christ all will be made alive."

Finally, listen to Jesus' own words in the Gospel of John 11:25, 26:

*"I am the resurrection and the life. He who believes in Me will live, even though he dies, and whoever lives and believes in Me will never die."*

# JESUS' ASCENSION

*Nay, Allah raised him up unto Himself:*
*and Allah is exalted in Power, Wise.*
Quran 4:158

*After the Lord Jesus had spoken to them, He was taken up*
*into heaven and He sat at the right hand of God.*
Mark 16:19

The quranic verse quoted above is astonishing in its admission that the Messiah was taken up to heaven. The details, as usual, vary greatly as to when this occurred. Leaving aside these differences, the passages from the Word of God that we would like to bring to the attention of our Muslim friends deal with exactly what Jesus' rank in heaven is and what is His function there.

Before getting to these points, invite your Muslim friend to read the following two accounts of Jesus ascending to heaven. The first is in Luke's gospel (Luke 24:50-52): "When He had led them out to the vicinity of Bethany [near Jerusalem], He lifted up his hands and blessed them. While He was blessing them, He left them and was taken up into heaven. Then they worshiped Him and returned to Jerusalem with great joy."

The account in the book of Acts gives a few more details (Acts 1:9-11):

After He said this, He was taken up before their very eyes, and a cloud hid Him from their sight. They were looking intently up into the sky as He was

31

going, when suddenly two men dressed in white stood beside them. "Men of Galilee," they said, "why do you stand here looking up into the sky? This same Jesus who has been taken from you into heaven, will come back in the same way you have seen Him go into heaven."

As interesting as these details are, the description of where He took up His position in heaven is far more interesting. He is not just "somehow there," He is at the right hand of God, a position of unbelievable power and, in one scene, at the very center of the throne. Invite your Muslim friend to look at these passages with you:

- "After the Lord Jesus had spoken to them, He was taken up into heaven and He sat *at the right hand of God*" (Mark 16:19).

- "[Jesus answered,] '[B]ut from now on, the Son of Man will be seated *at the right hand of The Mighty God*'" (Luke 22:69).

- "Then I [the Apostle John] saw a Lamb, looking as if it had been slain, standing *in the center of the throne*" (Revelation 5:6a) (all emphases added). Note that the Prophet John the Baptist referred to Jesus as "The Lamb of God." (John 1:29)

Jesus' position in heaven is one of extraordinary power at the right hand of the Mighty God, and His sacrificial death puts Him at the center of the throne as an atonement for sin.

Jesus' position endues Him with all the power of the Almighty. He will exercise that power one day as He deals with the people of the world who refused to bow to God, even as David prophesied in Psalm 2:9, "You will rule them with an iron scepter; You will dash them to pieces like pottery."

But there is another function of the One who sits at the right hand of Almighty God, and that is the role of Intercessor. By virtue of sacrificing Himself for our sins, He won the right to intercede on behalf of those who believed in God. Help your Muslim friend to find the following very interesting verses on this point.

In that great prophecy about Christ in the Prophet Isaiah (Isa. 52:13-53:12) is embedded this reference to His role as Intercessor:

> Therefore I [God] will give Him a portion among the great, and He will divide the spoils with the strong, because He poured out His life unto death, and was numbered with the transgressors. For He bore the sin of many and *made intercession for the transgressors* (Isa. 53:12) (emphasis added).

In his great treatise to the believers in Rome, the Apostle Paul explained Jesus' role: "Christ Jesus, who died—more than that, who was raised to life—is at the right hand of God and is also interceding for us" (Rom. 8:34).

The writer of the book entitled "Hebrews," explained this in terms of priesthood: "[B]ecause Jesus lives forever, He has a permanent priesthood. Therefore He is able to save completely those who come to God through Him, because He always lives to intercede for them" (Heb. 7:24, 25).

As you summarize all of this with your Muslim friend, you may want to point out:

- The Quran repeats what the Word of God stated six hundred years before the Quran existed.

- The Psalms, the Prophets and the Gospels contain

significant details that are not mentioned in the Quran.

- Jesus was awarded a position at the right hand of Almighty God, a position of great authority and power.

- By virtue of His sacrificial death on the cross, as the Lamb of God, Jesus won the right to intercede with our Father God on behalf of all who believe in Him.

- Jesus is going to return to the earth.

Dear Christian worker, by now you should be aware that these biblical accounts absolutely shatter the Muslim's preconceived ideas about what he or she has been taught concerning Jesus. The Quran and the *Hadith*, which are the written traditions of what Muhammad said and did and are outside of the Quran, give the impression that Jesus was a mere man for His age, not divine, not the eternal Son of God, not the Savior of the World and not an Intercessor. These new biblical insights for him or her may be most disturbing.

Be much in prayer as you work with your friend. Trust the Holy Spirit to bring conviction through your use of the Holy Scriptures, as we know them in the Bible. Be very loving and patient with your friend as he or she processes all these new revelations.

# JESUS' HONOR IN THIS WORLD AND THE NEXT

Muslims frequently say they honor Jesus more than we Christians do. This, by now often-quoted, verse, Quran 3:45, is one of the reasons they say this. Here it is again: "Behold! The angels said: 'O Mary! God giveth thee glad tidings of a Word from Him: his name will be Christ Jesus [*Isa al-Masih* in Arabic], the son of Mary, *held in honor in this world and the hereafter* and of (the company of) those nearest to God'" (emphasis added).

Let's engage our Muslim friends in this new idea that Jesus was "held in honor in this world and the hereafter," which is not explained in the Quran. During the days of His walk on earth, He indeed was honored above all men. Crowds of thousands gathered for His teaching. All who came to Him were healed. People were delivered from demons. His fame spread even to the king's palace. The common people loved Him.

In spite of His obvious goodness, demonstrated so openly in His healings, exorcisms, and forgiveness of peoples' sins, opposition developed among those who were jealous of His following. Eventually, Jewish leaders conspired to kill Him. Knowing all of this, Jesus made this unusual prophecy in John 12:32: "'But I, when I am lifted up from the earth, will draw all men to Myself.' He said this to show the kind of death [crucifixion] He was going to die."

Has this prophecy come true? Yes! By His death on the cross Jesus has already drawn millions and millions of believers to Himself. Ask your Muslim friend to think about these statistics. About 1,600,000,000 people are identified as Christians today. Even the Quran mentions Jesus' crucifixion. Muslims who believe in the crucifixion number about 1,500,000,000 people. Together, these two groups total almost half the population of the earth. Through Christian radio, films, video tapes, television, the internet, and the distribution of the printed scriptures in hundreds of languages, the story of Jesus' death on the cross has become known throughout many other parts of the world.

Truly, this prophecy of Jesus being honored in this world is being fulfilled right before our eyes. But what about the hereafter? The Scriptures have much to say about this. Seven hundred years before Jesus, Isaiah made this prophecy:

"For to us a child is born, to us a son is given, and the government will be on His shoulders. And He will be called Wonderful Counselor, Mighty God, Everlasting Father, Prince of Peace. Of the increase of His government and peace there will be no end. He will reign on David's throne and over his kingdom, establishing and upholding it with justice and righteousness from that time on and forever. The zeal of the LORD Almighty will accomplish this" (Isaiah 9:6-7).

This verse is about Jesus: God the Father will make His dwelling in Jesus by His Spirit. Here we see the oneness of God: Father, Son and Spirit, and the eternity of God's rule.

In the book of Zechariah 9:9b (one of the biblical prophets), approximately five hundred years before Christ, this prophecy was made, "See, your *king* comes to you, righteous and having salvation, gentle and riding on a donkey, on a colt, the foal of a donkey."

This was fulfilled in Jesus' day. With your Muslim friend please read the passage from Luke 19:28-38. Jesus is acclaimed King as he enters Jerusalem for the last time, riding on a donkey.

Pontius Pilate, the Roman governor of Jerusalem, asked Jesus before His crucifixion, "Are you the king of the Jews?" After Jesus' affirmative reply, the governor stated, "You are a king then!" And Jesus answered him in this way (John 18:37): "You are right in saying I am a king. In fact, for this reason I was born, and for this I came into the world to testify to the truth. Everyone on the side of truth listens to Me."

Now please read John 19. Jesus, the King, was crucified and buried. Next read John 20 and Acts 1:1-11. On the third day, just as Jesus had prophesied, He rose from the dead, showed Himself alive to many for the next forty days, and then ascended to heaven. But there is more. To the Apostle John were given visions of future events. We will quote from one of them, Revelation 19:11, 13, 16, which shows His position in the "hereafter": "I saw heaven standing open and there before me was a white horse, whose rider is called Faithful and True.... His name is the Word of God.... On His robe and on His thigh He has this name written: *King of Kings and Lord of Lords*" (emphasis added).

This is Jesus, held in honor in this world and the hereafter!

# JESUS' RETURN

*And (Jesus) shall be a sign (for the coming of) the Hour (Of Judgment)*
Quran 43:61

*That day will bring about the destruction of the heavens by fire, and the elements will melt in the heat. But in keeping with His promise we are looking forward to a new heaven and a new earth, the home of righteousness.*
2 Peter 3:12, 13

All Muslims believe that Jesus is alive in heaven right now and that He will return. But that's as far as the similarity goes. According to Muslim traditions, our friends have been taught that Jesus will return as a Muslim; He will break all the crosses in the world; He will kill all the pigs in the world; He will help convert the whole world to Islam, will marry, have children and die as a normal human being. These are not teachings taken from the Quran but have been taken from the *Hadith*, that is, the things that Muhammad said outside of the Quran.

Over and over, Muhammad returned to the theme of "the Day of Doom." In another passage, Muhammad caught the imagery of power that will characterize Jesus' return: "When the earth is pounded to powder, and thy Lord cometh, and His angels, rank upon rank, and Hell, that Day, is brought (face to face), —On that Day will man remember..." (Quran 89:21-23).

How sad that Muhammad, in questioning Christians

concerning what they believed, got only the judgment element in the prophecy and missed the promise of unutter-
able joy for those who believed in Jesus as the Son of God,
sent by God the Father. We will look at both aspects of
Jesus' return.

First, invite your Muslim friend to read a fuller description in the Bible of what the Quran hinted at. Look together at the end-time passage in the Gospel of Matthew
24:27-31:

> [A]s the lightning that comes from the East is visible
> even in the West, so will be the coming of the Son of
> Man [one of Jesus' names]... '[T]he sun will be dark-
> ened, and the moon will not give its light; the stars
> will fall from the sky, and the heavenly bodies will
> be shaken.' [A]ll the nations of the earth will mourn.
> They will see the Son of Man coming on the clouds
> of the sky, with power and great glory. And He will
> send His angels with a loud trumpet call, and they
> shall gather His elect...

This is a fuller picture of what Muhammad was referring to in the Quran. Not only will Jesus come in this
way, but He will come to judge. Have your friend read Acts
17:31, "For He [God] has set a day when He will judge the
world with justice by the man He has appointed [that is,
Christ Jesus]. He [God] has given proof of this to all men by
raising Him [Christ Jesus] from the dead."

Having shown, with the above scriptural passages, a
fuller picture of what Muhammad was referring to, turn
now to the biblical material concerning Jesus' first appearance on the earth, not His last. In the Gospel of John, Jesus
explains His mission. Have your friend read with you John
3:16-21:

For God so loved the world that He gave His one and only Son, that whoever believes in Him shall not perish but have eternal life. For God did not send His Son into the world to condemn the world, but to save the world through Him. Whoever believes in Him is not condemned, but whoever does not believe stands condemned already because he has not believed in the name of God's one and only Son. This is the verdict: Light has come into the world [Jesus is called "the Light of the World," John 8:12], but men loved darkness instead of light because their deeds were evil. Everyone who does evil hates the light, and will not come into the light for fear that his deeds will be exposed. But whoever lives by the truth comes into the light, so that it may be seen plainly that what he has done has been done through God.

From the above, it can be seen that what you believe about Jesus' work on earth, when He came the first time, has everything to do with how you will view His final appearing. When you believe in Jesus Christ as Lord and Savior, yes, even as the Son of God, then your attitude will be one of joyous expectation, not of fear of judgment. Have your friend read the Apostle Paul's words in Philippians 3:20, 21, "[O]ur citizenship is in heaven. And we eagerly await a Savior from there, the Lord Jesus Christ, who by the power that enables Him to bring everything under His control, will transform our lowly bodies so that they will be like His glorious [incorruptible] body."

Long ago, the Prophet David understood this and believed in the One to come. This is what he wrote: "You have made known to me the path of life; You will fill me with joy in Your presence, with eternal pleasures at Your right hand" Psalm 16:11.

On the one hand, the return of Christ is to be feared by those who have rejected Him, because He is God's Son, our Lord and our Savior. On the other hand, for those who love Him, there is cause for great joy when He shall appear. God gave the Apostle John a glimpse of the future with Christ. He wrote in Revelation 21:3, 4:

> I heard a loud voice from the throne saying, "Now the dwelling of God is with men, and He will live with them. They will be His people, and God Himself will be with them and be their God. He will wipe away every tear from their eyes. There will be no more death or mourning or crying or pain, for the old order of things has passed away."

Dear Christian worker, invite your Muslim friend to receive Christ, to believe on Him for who He really is. I suggest 1 John 5:11-13 as one of several passages to use for this:

*This is the testimony: God has given us eternal life, and this life is in His Son. He who has the Son has life; he who does not have the Son of God does not have life. I write these things to you who believe in the name of the Son of God so that you may know that you have eternal life.*

# JESUS'
# MIRACLES

# JESUS MADE THE BLIND TO SEE

Not so long ago, I was invited to be part of a panel discussion at Texas A&M University. The topic was "Muhammad in the Bible." The chief Muslim spokesman was Dr. Jamal Badawi, the author of the book by the same title (1982).

The Christian reader may be surprised to learn that one of the biblical passages that Muslims claim refers to Muhammad is Deuteronomy 18:18. It reads, "I [God] will raise up for them [the people of God] a prophet like you [Moses] from among their brothers [the twelve tribes of Israel; I will put my words in his mouth, and he will tell them everything I command him." In spite of the fact that this passage is clearly applied to Jesus (who is descended from the tribe of Judah) by Peter in Acts 3:22, and Stephen in Acts 7:37, Muslims claim this prophecy for Muhammad. Using the above passage from Deuteronomy, Dr. Badawi showed, in his opinion, several ways in which Muhammad resembled Moses and Jesus did not. For example, Moses and Muhammad were both married, gave to the world a body of Law and led victorious armies. He pointed out that Jesus did none of the above.

For the Christian who knows the biblical accounts of Moses and Jesus, the glaring differences between Muhammad and Jesus are in the area of sacrifices and miracles. With one lone exception from Quran 37:107, there are no other references in the Quran to sacrifices, whereas Moses' teaching is filled with laws regarding many kinds of sacrifices, and Jesus Himself came to be a sacrifice. With regard to miracles, both Moses and Jesus performed numerous outstanding miracles. Muhammad claimed his only miracle was the Quran itself. In other words, he performed no miracles. For this study, we are going to focus on the area of Jesus' miracle in *healing the blind* for reasons that will become apparent.

Amazingly, the Quran makes two outstanding references to this. In Quran 3:49, it says, "...I [Jesus] heal those born blind,..." And in Q. 5:113, supposedly, God says, in speaking to Jesus, "By My leave...thou healest those born blind..." And that's all. In the Quran, there is not a single story of Jesus actually giving sight to a blind person.

An approach that we will use often in working with our Muslim friends goes something like this: "Abdullah, I have read in the Quran that Jesus healed the blind, but there is not one description of Him actually doing this. I have found in the ancient book of Jesus a detailed account of Him actually healing a man born blind. Would you like to read the story?"

Remember, the quranic references cited above serve as stepping stones, or starting points, to lead your friend to the original source material in the Bible. There are several stories of Jesus healing the blind (Matt. 9:27-31, Matt. 20:30-34, Mark 8:22-26, Mark 10:46-52). In this study we are going to use the one in John 9:1-41, because it refers to a man born blind. Please, if you can, put the Bible or the New Testament in the hands of your Muslim friend and have him or her read this passage. There are many startling new things that your Muslim friend has never read or heard before about Jesus.

Then, call attention to the fact that this miracle is a stunning display of God's love, mercy and power working through Jesus:

1. The purpose of Jesus' miracle was to display the love of God (v. 3).

2. Jesus, in this story, called Himself, "The Light of the World" (v. 5).

3. The healed man initially said that Jesus was a prophet (v. 17).

4. The healed man said, "This man [Jesus] is from God" (v. 33).

5. The healed man believed Jesus was "the Son of Man" (vv. 35-38). Jesus is called "Son of God" in Scripture (Matthew 3:17), and claimed equality with God (John 10:30 and 14:9), but He more frequently referred to Himself as "the Son of Man." Remember, He died for us on the cross *as representative man*; but because He was also the Son of God, His sacrifice was of infinite worth, sufficient to cover the sins of the whole world.

6. The healed man finally called Jesus "Lord," and worshiped Him (v.38).

7. Also remember that Jesus giving sight to the blind is a fulfillment of Old Testament prophecies: Isaiah 29:18; 35:5; and 42:7.

Friend, in your own loving way, open your Muslim friend's eyes to what the real Word of God says about Jesus and prepare yourself to patiently answer the many questions that are going to arise. How you handle yourself is part of your witness.

# JESUS THE HEALER

The Quran tantalizes us with minimal references, and no stories to reflect the glory of the Father as He worked miracles of healing through His Son Jesus Christ.

In Quran 3:49, we read (supposedly, Jesus is speaking), "I heal...the lepers."

And in Quran 5:110, we read (God supposedly is speaking to Jesus), "By my leave, thou healest...the lepers." That's it. Nowhere in the Quran do you find the rich material concerning leprosy such as in the Law of Moses, nor any of the narratives of Jesus actually healing a leper.

Jesus' miracles of healing are an attestation to His divine Messiahship and the actual presence of the kingdom of God on earth. By contrast, Muhammad admitted in the Quran that he himself had no miracles (Quran 6:109; 10:20; 13:7 and 17:59).

So, my dear Christian friend, as you sit with your Muslim neighbor and discuss the whole issue of healing, remember that the Quran itself claims to confirm the law of Moses, the Psalms of David, the Prophets and the Good News of Jesus Christ. Quran 29:46 reads, "We believe in the Revelation which has come down to us and in that which came down to you..."

With this in mind, you may want to ask your Muslim friend if he or she would like to find out what Moses said about leprous people. By now, you should have your Bible open to Leviticus 13:45-46, which reveals the horrible plight of lepers: "The person with such an infectious disease must wear torn clothes, let his hair be unkempt, cover the lower part of his face and cry out, 'Unclean! Unclean!'...He must live alone; he must live outside the camp."

You may also want to take your Muslim friend to the amazing story of Moses being called to become a prophet. When Moses was asking the Lord how the people would believe that God had sent him, the Lord gave an amazing sign. Have your friend read Exodus 4:6-7:

> Then the Lord said, "Put your hand inside your cloak." So Moses put his hand into his cloak, and when he took it out, it was leprous, like snow. "Now put it back into your cloak," He said. So Moses put his hand back into his cloak, and when he took it out, it was restored like the rest of his flesh."

Please point out to your friend that this is something that only God could do. When we get to Jesus' miracles, they attest to His deity.

In Leviticus 14:1-32 (in the Law of Moses), we read of an astonishing procedure that a person must go through when he or she is cleansed of leprosy. In this short study, we cannot quote the whole passage; but we can note items of extreme interest. For example, the healed person is to bring to the priests for sacrifice two unblemished male lambs and a ewe lamb. One lamb is to be offered as a guilt offering. Another is to be offered as a sin offering, and the third as a burnt offering. Blood is to be put on the right ear, thumb and big toe of the healed persons, along with oil, and more is poured over the head of the healed person. These are to make atonement for that person before the Lord.

You, the Christian worker, should familiarize yourself with this passage and engage your Muslim friend in reading it with you. There are many more actions that are prescribed, but we have highlighted that which so clearly points to the atoning sacrifice of Jesus, namely, the shedding of the blood of the Lamb.

You need to know that the Quran teaches no one can make atonement for another. See Quran 10:54, "Every soul that hath sinned, if it possessed all that is on earth, would fain give it in ransom..." In Islam, no ransom, no atonement. So this discussion of being atoned for by the blood of a lamb is a new idea for the Muslim.

Since the Quran also affirms what was revealed to the biblical prophets (Quran 3:84), it is appropriate to introduce your friend to the prophecy of the suffering of God's servant in Isaiah 53:5, "But He was pierced for our transgressions, He was crushed for our iniquities; the punishment that brought us peace was upon Him, and by His wounds we are healed." (You may want to read this whole biblical chapter.)

Now when we come to a Gospel/*Injil* story of Jesus healing a leper, for example, in Matthew 8:3, Jesus simply says, "'Be clean!' Immediately he was cured of his leprosy."

You will need to explain to your Muslim friend that Jesus did not have this divine power to cure leprosy as a mere prophet, but that He won that right to heal all of our diseases by sacrificing Himself on the cross as an atonement for all of our sins. "By his wounds we are healed." God the Father, knowing in advance that Jesus was going to sacrifice Himself as the Lamb of God, gave Him this authority to heal.

Dear Christian friend, take this information, familiarize yourself with it, expand it and help your Muslim friend appreciate Jesus as the Divine Healer.

## JESUS RAISES THE DEAD

This stepping stone has to do with Jesus' miracle of raising the dead. Quran 5:110 reads in part, "...I strengthened thee with the Holy Spirit...and behold! Thou bringest forth the dead by my leave." Unfortunately, there is not a single story in the Quran of Jesus doing so. Therefore, we turn to the Gospel for a story of Jesus actually raising someone from the dead.

It is at this point that we ask our Muslim friend if he or she would like to read an account of Jesus raising a man who had been dead for four days. (Be persuasive.) By now you should have your Bible open to John chapter 11: have your friend read John 11:1-44.

This may be the first time your Muslim friend has ever read the Bible. In this passage there are going to be many shocks for him or her. The Muslim has been taught that Jesus was only a mere man for His age and that He was not the Son of God. Nor has the Muslim ever linked the quranic word *Al-Masih* (Arabic, "Messiah" for us) with the Son of God. Here they are linked in verse 27.

Other interesting points are that Jesus loved Lazarus. He wept with the sisters and friends. He prayed to God in heaven, whom He called "Father." He thanked the Father for hearing His prayer for Lazarus to be raised. And He called Himself "the resurrection and the life." He promised that whoever believed in Him, even if he died, he would live. These are all fascinating new thoughts for your Muslim friend. They not only show Jesus in a very loving human way, but they also reveal that Jesus made startling claims for Himself and allowed Himself to be called the Son of God (verses 4 and 27).

Because the Muslim has been taught that Jesus is not the Son of God, you may have to take time to deal with this. You may have to point out that we Christians do not believe what Muslims think we do. They have been taught that when we say, "Jesus is the Son of God," we believe that God had sex with Mary. There is not a Christian anywhere in the world that believes this.

There are passages that talk about Jesus' relationship with the Father. For example, John 6:38, "For I [Jesus] have come down from heaven...to do the will of Him [the Father] who sent Me," and John 14:9, "He who has seen Me has seen the Father," and John 10:30, "I and the Father are one." These verses are very important for Muslims because they teach the oneness of God—a key tenet of Muslim faith. Muslims are surprised when they discover that we, too, believe God is one.

Remember, they have never read the Bible before. They have never been taught that God is their Father. It is your privilege to show them. Deut. 32:6, "...O foolish and unwise people...Is He not your Father, your Creator, who made you and formed you?" But in addition to this, you will have to show them that Jesus came to reveal the Father, to show the world what God is like.

In the story of Jesus raising Lazarus, we learn that our Father God, being one with Jesus, loved Lazarus through Jesus. And Jesus used this miracle to glorify the Father and offer eternal life to all who believe in Him, the one whom the Father sent.

# JESUS' EARTHLY ROLES

# JESUS AS A PROPHET

The Quran has nine references where Jesus is listed, or alluded to, as a prophet along with other biblical prophets. In Quran 19:30, where we see Jesus referred to as a servant, we also read that He is called a prophet: "He said[1]: 'I am indeed a servant of God: He hath given me Revelation[2] and made me a prophet.'"

The idea in both the Bible and the Quran is that a prophet was chosen for a special purpose with a message from God. The Quran mentions that the name of Jesus' book is "the Gospel," and it also mentions His miracles and that He confirmed the books that came before Him: the Law of Moses, the Psalms of David, and the earlier Prophets (see Quran 5:48). But the Quran mentions *nothing* of His teaching or futuristic prophecies.

In the Bible, we learn that Jesus fulfilled all the concepts of Priesthood, Kingship, and Prophethood. In this study, let us try to uncover what they might mean with regard to Prophethood.

The word "prophet" means someone who speaks on behalf of God because he "hears" in his inner being what God is saying to him. We see this in Jesus' life. With your Muslim friend, please read Jesus' own words in John 7:16 and John 8:26, respectively: "My teaching is not My own. It comes from Him who sent Me." "He who sent Me is reli-

---

[1] Here Jesus is speaking from His cradle, according to the Quran.

[2] Here "Revelation" should have been translated "The Book," *Al-Kitab* in Arabic.

able, and what I have heard from Him I tell the world."

From this, we conclude that all that Jesus taught is from God the Father. When we read His beautiful, ethical teaching, we are amazed at how different it is from that of the world. For example, with regard to cruel treatment from fellow human beings, He taught, "Love your enemies, do good to those who hate you, bless those who curse you, pray for those who mistreat you," (Luke 6:27). And with regard to God, He taught, "Love the Lord your God with all your heart and with all your soul and with all your mind," (Matt. 22:37, also found in the Law of Moses, Deut. 6:5).

Biblical prophets also foretold the future. We see this in Jesus' teaching as well. For example, He foretold the destruction of the Temple in Matthew 24:2: "I tell you the truth, not one stone here will be left on another; every one will be thrown down." This was fulfilled *40 years after Jesus died*, when the Roman general Titus destroyed the Temple in 70 A.D.

But there is more. Earlier, Jesus had made this shattering prophecy to the rebellious Jews in Matthew 21:43: "The Kingdom of God will be taken away from you [the Jews] and given to a [non-Jewish] people who will produce its fruit."

During the final Jewish rebellion, 133-135 A.D., all Jerusalem was leveled. The Jewish state was no more. This marked the end of the Jewish people's aspiration to be the Kingdom of God. From that time on, the stewardship of preaching and teaching the Kingdom of God passed to the Gentile believers, those from non-Jewish nations.

In addition to the above, Jesus also prophesied His own destruction and resurrection. Have your Muslim friend look at this passage, Mathew 20:17-19, with you:

> Now as Jesus was going up to Jerusalem, He took the twelve disciples aside and said to them, "We are going up to Jerusalem, and the Son of Man will be betrayed to the chief priests and the teachers of the law. They will condemn Him to death and turn Him over to the Gentiles to be mocked and flogged and crucified. On the third day He will be raised up to life!"

Now take your Muslim friend through Isaiah 53 and match the prophecies there with the fulfillment of many of those found in Matthew 26:47-28:15 and Luke 24:1-26:

- Jesus was betrayed by one of His own disciples, Judas Iscariot (use Psalm 41:9).

- Jesus was taken before the high priests and the teachers of the law and the elders.

- They asked, "Are you the Christ, the Son of God?"

- Jesus answered that, yes, He was.

- Jesus was crucified between two thieves where He died on the cross.

- On the third day after His burial, He was raised from the dead.

- The resurrected Christ explained to His disciples that all that the prophets had spoken had to be fulfilled, namely, that Christ would suffer these things and enter into His glory.

Lastly, we read that Jesus prophesied His sending of the Holy Spirit in John 14:15-17a: "If you love Me you will obey what I command. And I will ask the Father, and He will give you another Counselor to be with you forever— the Spirit of Truth."

This was fulfilled on the Day of Pentecost, *ten days after Jesus had ascended* to heaven (Acts 2:1-41). This same Holy Spirit is promised to all who repent of their sins and believe in the Lord Jesus Christ.

# JESUS AS A SIGN TO THE WORLD

*The people walking in darkness have seen a great light; on those living in the land of the shadow of death a light has dawned.*
Isaiah 9:2

The verse above is taken from that great prophecy in Isaiah on the birth of Jesus (Isaiah 9:1-7). The verse we are going to look at in the Quran is also about the birth of Jesus: "We breathed into her [the Virgin Mary] of our Spirit, and we made her and her Son a sign for all peoples" (Quran 21:91).

Nowhere in the Quran do we read of how Jesus was to be a sign for all the peoples of the world. All that your Muslim friends know is that He was given a book called the *Injil*, which supposedly was only for guidance to the Jewish people of his day. But that comes short of the mark, doesn't it?

Let's look at this Arabic word *Injil* for a moment. It is an Arabic corruption of the Greek word *euangelion*, which means "good news." Some Muslim scholars know this, but the average Muslim thinks *Injil* is merely the title of the book that God gave to Jesus. It will be your privilege to explain to your Muslim friend what this word actually means. When you do, it raises the question, what is this "good news?"

Our first clue comes from the story of the angels appearing to shepherds on the hills outside of Bethlehem announcing the birth of Jesus (Luke 2:10-11a). Please have

61

your Muslim friend read this verse: "The angel said to them, 'Do not be afraid. I bring you good news of great joy that will be *for all the people*. Today in the town of David [Bethlehem] a *Savior* has been born to you..." (emphasis added).

As you read this with your Muslim friend, you will want to emphasize that Jesus, who was virgin-born, truly was God's miraculous "sign" to all the people of the world. He was a sign that God had heard the cry of the world's peoples for mercy. As the angel of the Lord explained to Joseph (who would later wed Mary), Jesus was going to be a *Savior*. With your Muslim friend please read this verse from Matthew: "She will give birth to a son, and you are to give Him the name Jesus because He will save His people from their sins" (Matt. 1:21).

To those sitting "in the land of the shadow of death," Jesus' coming into the world truly is "good news." In teaching precepts to his young disciple, Timothy, the Apostle Paul expressed it this way (1 Tim. 1:15): "Here is a trustworthy saying that deserves full acceptance: Christ Jesus [*Isa al-Masih* in Arabic] came into the world to save sinners..."

Jesus in His own words explains His purpose in coming into the world (Luke 19:10), "The Son of Man came to seek and to save what was lost."

How Jesus was going to do this is the most important question of this study. Let's look at another passage where Jesus foretells this (John 12:32, 33), "'But I, when I am lifted up from the earth, will draw all men to Myself.' He said this to show the kind of death He was going to die."

Jesus prophesied that He would be crucified. This is

why God sent Him into the world.

This was to be the "sign" for all the peoples of the world. God sent His Son to be the sacrificial "Lamb of God who would take away the sin of the world." Other apostles testify to this. Please read what the Apostle Paul wrote in 2 Corinthians 5:21, "God made Him who had no sin to be sin for us, so that in Him we might become the righteousness of God."

And as the Apostle Peter stated it (1 Peter 2:24a), "He Himself bore our sins in His own body on the tree [the cross], so that we might die to sins and live for righteousness."

In the last book of the Bible, all of this reaches a grand climax in the scenes revealed to the Apostle John. Turn with your Muslim friend to Revelation 5:6-9 and read:

> Then I saw a Lamb, looking as if it had been slain, standing in the center of the throne... [T]he elders fell down before the Lamb.... [a]nd they sang a new song: "You are worthy to take the scroll and open its seals, because You were slain, and with Your blood You purchased men for God from every tribe and language and people and nation."

Truly, Jesus' birth, His coming into the world to save all who would believe in Him, was a great sign. His birth was the sign that sin would be finished, death overcome, and eternal life given to all who believed in Him.

# JESUS AS A WITNESS

In Quran 5:117, we find another one of those descriptive names that is given to Jesus—He is called "a witness." But no explanation is given of what He was witnessing to. Before we ask our Muslim friend to look into the ancient texts with us to find out what Jesus was bearing witness to, let's have a look at this quranic verse[1], "Never said I to them aught except what Thou didst command me to say, to wit, 'Worship Allah [God] my Lord and your Lord;' and I was a witness over them whilst I dwelt amongst them..."

The beauty of this stepping stone is that it opens the door to the whole life and ministry of Jesus! His entire ministry was a witness to how God looks at everything. Let's have a look at how Jesus explained Himself to His own generation: "For I did not speak of My own accord, but the Father who sent Me commanded Me what to say and how to say it. I know that His command leads to eternal life. So whatever I say is just what the Father has told Me to say" (John 12:49-50).

Your Muslim friend has never thought of God as Father. In fact, he or she may have been taught that it is improper to think of God that way. Just remind your friend that from the beginning God, in the Law of Moses, revealed Himself to us as Father (Deut. 32:6b, "Is He not your Father, your Creator, who made you and formed you?").

Thus, we see that God our Father sent Jesus to reveal His thoughts. This would include God's evaluation of

---

[1] Supposedly, Jesus is speaking.

the world of rebellious men and women. Please read John 7:7 wherein Jesus is speaking, "...I testify [bear witness] that what it [the world] does is evil." The scripture describes the world in 1 John 2:16 as follows: "For everything in the world—the cravings of sinful man, the lust of his eyes and the boasting of what he has and does—comes not from the Father but from the world."

But Jesus also came to bear witness to God's love and to live it out. In 1 John 4:8, 16, we read these amazing words, "God is love." We see His love manifested in so many ways. With your Muslim friend, review these following passages that show how Jesus testified to the reality of God's love. Take your time as you sit with your Muslim friend and look up these references and ponder them and meditate on how great the love of God is in sending Jesus as His witness. Remember that Jesus said He only did what He saw the Father doing (John 5:19). He was a living witness of God in loving and compassionate action among men, women and children.

- He raised Lazarus from the dead (John 11:1-44).

- He gave sight to a man born blind (John 9:1-33).

- He healed lepers (Matthew 8:2-3).

- He delivered people from demons and healed all the sick (Matthew 8:16).

- He loved little children (Mark 10:13-16).

- He fed thousands who were hungry (Matthew 14:13-21).

- He showed how much He loved His disciples by washing their feet (John 13:5).

- He forgave the sins of a woman caught in adultery (John 8:3-11).

- He forgave His enemies who were crucifying Him (Luke 23:34).

- He gave eternal life to all who believed in Him (Mark 10:29-30).

Jesus came into the world as a witness to the love of God. While He was free to minister, He testified by miracle after miracle what the love of God was like. But as Jesus prepared to leave the world, He bore witness to the love of God for lost mankind in another, astounding way. Let's turn to passages that His beloved disciple John wrote long after Jesus had ascended to heaven (1 John 4:9-10, 14-17):

This is how God showed His love among us: He sent His one and only Son into the world that we might live through Him. This is love: not that we loved God but that He loved us and sent His Son *as an atoning sacrifice for our sins.*

And we have seen and testify that the Father has sent the Son to be *the Savior of the world.* If anyone acknowledges that Jesus is the Son of God, God lives in him and he in God. And so we know and rely on the love God has for us. God is love. Whoever lives in love lives in God, and God in him. In this way, love is made complete among us so that we will have *confidence on the day of judgment..."* (emphasis added).

The cross was the ultimate expression of His witness! It witnessed to what God thought of sin: "The wages of sin is death" (Romans 6:23). Jesus was crucified for our sins. On the cross Jesus bore witness to the extent of God's love for humanity: "[Y]ou were redeemed from the empty way of life handed down to you from your forefathers...with the precious blood of Christ..." (1 Peter 1:18-19). He saved us from judgment. He became our Savior.

But He became much more. In the last book of the Bible, we read these words: "Grace and peace to you...from Jesus Christ who is the faithful witness, the firstborn from the dead, and the ruler of the kings of the earth" (Revelation 1:4-6).

Just think about that! Jesus, the faithful witness, was raised from the dead to become the ruler of the kings of the earth.

*"To Him be glory and power for ever and ever."* Amen.

# JESUS AS A MESSENGER

The word "messenger" in the Arabic Quran is "*rasul.*" It means "one who is sent." This word is often translated as "Apostle." For the purpose of this study, we are choosing to use the meaning "one who is sent." Let us look at couple of verses in the Quran that mention Jesus as a Messenger, "a Sent One":

> We gave Moses the Book and followed him up with a succession of Messengers [sent ones]; We gave Jesus the Son of Mary clear (signs) and strengthened him with the holy spirit" (Quran 2:87).

> And then in their wake [Noah, Abraham and other prophets], We followed them up with Our Messengers [sent ones]: We sent after them Jesus the son of Mary, and bestowed on him The Gospel; and We ordained in the hearts of those who followed Him Compassion and Mercy (Quran 57:27).

Ten times in the Quran Jesus is referred to as a *rasul,* "Sent One," "Messenger" or "Apostle." In summarizing the thoughts of the two above verses, the picture that the Muslim reader gets is that Jesus was a "Sent One," who was given clear signs (miracles) by God, was strengthened by the Holy Spirit, and given The Gospel (The Good News).

That is the gist of what the Quran says about Jesus as a Messenger, "a Sent One."

In the light of what we know from the gospel accounts, notice what is left out. The above quranic verses do not indicate that it was the Father who sent Him, nor what His mission was. Please invite your Muslim friend to look with you in the Gospels to learn, in Jesus' own words, what His mission was and how He explained Himself to His generation. Let's start with Jesus' words in John 6:38-40:

> "For I have come down from heaven not to do My will but to do the will of Him who sent Me. And this is the will of Him who sent Me, that I should lose none of all that He has given Me, but raise them up at the last day. For My Father's will is that everyone who looks to the Son and believes in Him shall have eternal life, and I will raise him up at the last day."

There is so much packed into these simple words of Jesus. Let's try to highlight them:

- Jesus came down from heaven.

- His mission was to do the will of the Father and that meant that He would lose none that God the Father gave Him.

- He is going to raise them up from the dead on that day that He returns.

- God the Father's will is that everyone who looks to Jesus as the Son of God and believes in Him shall have eternal life and will be raised up on the last day.

When Jesus said that He came down (was sent down) from heaven, He is referring to His pre-existence from all eternity as God's Son. Let's look at Hebrews 1:3, where we read, "The Son is the radiance of God's glory and the exact representation of His being..."

This is the Eternal God, who was called our Father in the Law of Moses (Deuteronomy 32:6), who chose to express Himself through His Eternal Word. And in John 1:1-3 and 14, God the Word became flesh in the form of Jesus. As God's representative, He was full of grace and truth and He made God known (John 1:18) because God, in His love, wanted to make Himself known.

The mission of Jesus was to save all the people God the Father gave to Him. Remember, *Isa* in the Quran was actually called *Yeshua* in the original language of the Bible, and this is a word that means "Savior." Jesus, the Messenger, was sent as a Savior to save God's people from their sins and the subsequent penalty of death and hell. God did this because He loved us. For the Bible says God is love (1 John 4:8,16). Jesus, who represents God the Father, is therefore love-in-action, carrying out the Father's will. In love Jesus gave Himself as a ransom for us all.

The second purpose of Jesus was to give us eternal life, which meant He would raise us up on the Last Day, give us victory over sin and death so that we could live in the presence of God our Father for all eternity.

To do this, Jesus had to conquer death. The Gospel teaches us that "the wages of sin is death" (Rom. 6:23). Jesus came to die for us, to die in our place, to pay that penalty for all of us. If He were only a human man, maybe His sacrifice could be made for one other person. But if He were the Son of God, who came from the Father, and was one with the Father, His sacrifice would be of infinite worth. It would be sufficient to cover the sins of the whole world. This is what the Apostle John[1] wrote: "He is the atoning sacrifice for our sins, and not only for ours, but also for the sins of the whole world" (1 John 2:2).

---

[1] Not John the Baptist, but one of Jesus' twelve Apostles.

One other point to ponder is this: If Jesus were a mere man and He were to die, then He would not be there to carry us with Him into eternity. But if He really is the Eternal Son of God, in total oneness with God the Father, then He will be there for all eternity for all of us who believe in Him. Dear Friend, read how the Apostle John put it in John 1:12-13: "[T]o all who received Him, to those who believed in His name, He gave the right to become children of God—children born not of natural descent, nor of human decision or a husband's will, but born of God." This then truly is the Gospel, the Good News.

# JESUS AS REVELATION (THE BOOK)

The Quran is so rich in stepping stones: references to Jesus that always lead back to the original source material in the Word of God; words that illuminate that which is obscure and ultimately lead the believing reader to eternal truths.

Quran 19:30 states[1], "I am indeed a servant of God: He hath given me *Revelation* [the actual word in Arabic is *Al-Kitab*, meaning *The Book*] and made me a prophet" (emphasis added).

"*Injil*" is the quranic name for the book that God supposedly gave to Jesus. In another study, we show how "*Injil*" is an Arabic version of the Greek word "*euanggelion*," which means "Good News." How felicitous. Our Muslim friends believe God gave Jesus a book called "the Good News." In the Revised A. Yusuf Ali translation of the Quran which we are using, we find a supporting verse (Q. 57:27) that says "We[2]...bestowed on him [Jesus] The Gospel [Arabic '*Injil*'].

What a joy it will be to invite your Muslim friend on a guided tour of ancient scriptures to discover several facets of how this jeweled word "gospel" or "good news" is used. Help your Muslim friend find the following references and read them together.

---

[1] Supposedly Jesus is speaking as a babe in His mother's arms.
[2] Supposedly, God is speaking.

Let's start with Mark 1:15: "The time has come....The Kingdom of God is near. Repent and believe the *good news* [the gospel]" (emphasis added). What a wake-up call this is to Jesus' audience and to those who read these words today. Jesus came to introduce the Kingdom of God. It would not be of this world, as Jesus explained to the Roman governor (John 18:36), because this world is passing away (1 John 2:17) and that which is permanent will remain (Heb. 12:28, the unshakeable kingdom of God). Jesus asked His audience to repent of following the ways of this world and seek their citizenship in the kingdom of God (Matt. 6:33).

Now let's take a glimpse into Jesus' ministry to see what He preached and did. Please turn with your Muslim friend to Matthew 4:23: "Jesus went throughout Galilee, teaching in their synagogues [gathering places], preaching the good news of the kingdom, and healing every disease and sickness among the people." The new element here is that the kingdom of God is characterized by the healing of all the diseases afflicting mankind. And there is more. In Matthew 8:16, we read, "[M]any who were demon-possessed were brought to Him, and He drove out the [evil] spirits with a word..."

The good news is that people are going to be healed and delivered from the affliction of demons. These will be the marks of the kingdom of God here on earth.

There are more facets of this "good news," this gospel. Remember the story of Jesus' birth? What did the angel say to the shepherds? "...I bring you *good news* of great joy.... Today...a *Savior* has been born to you; He is *Christ the Lord*" (Luke 2:10-11) (emphasis added). In addition to healing and casting out demons, Christ is going to be a *Savior* – saving us from the consequences of our sins and even from death itself, and He will be called "*Lord.*"

74

This book, then, the one mentioned in the Quran that was supposedly given to Jesus, the one called "the Good News" or the "Gospel," "*Injil*" in Arabic, is not a book that Jesus was to teach to His generation, but rather it is a book about His life and ministry here on earth. To summarize it in all its rich details in this brief space is impossible. But the part that has to do with our salvation from sin and death was put into a formula that the Apostle Paul quoted: "By this *gospel* you are saved...[W]hat I received I passed on to you as of first importance: that *Christ died for our sins* according to the Scriptures, that *He was buried*, [and] that *He was raised on the third day* according to the Scriptures" (1 Cor. 15:2-4) (emphasis added). No doubt, you will want to read the rich details of how He died and was raised again. May we suggest that, together with your Muslim friend, you read Matthew 26-28. It will take time, but the Scripture is its own best interpreter. Highlight the following:

- Jesus prophesied His own crucifixion (Matt. 26:2, 21).

- Jesus gave the ceremony of bread and wine as symbols of His broken body and shed blood as signs of His eternal covenant with those who believed (Matt. 26:26-28). He recommended it be observed until His return to earth (1 Cor. 11:26).

- During His trial, Jesus admitted that He was the Christ [the Messiah, *Al-Masih*] and the Son of God, the one sent by God the Father, who would return to the Father after His mission of providing eternal life for all who believed on Him was done. (Mark 14:61, 62; John 17:20-26.)

On the cross, Jesus paid the penalty for all our sins, tasted death for every man, and then rose victorious from the grave to be alive forevermore. From the Father in heaven, He received authority over everything in heaven and on earth. He is with us always, even to the end of the age (Matt. 28:18-20).

"Christ Jesus...has destroyed death and has brought life and immortality to light through the gospel," the Good News, the *Injil* (2 Tim. 1:10). *Al-humdalillah*, praise the Lord.

# JESUS' TABLE FROM HEAVEN

*Behold! the Disciples said: "O Jesus the son of
Mary! Can thy Lord send down to us a table
set (with viands) from heaven?" Said Jesus:
"Fear Allah, if you have faith." They said: "We
only wish to eat thereof and satisfy our hearts,
and to know that thou hast indeed told us the
truth; and that we ourselves be witnesses to the
miracle." Said Jesus the son of Mary: "O Allah
our Lord! Send us from heaven a table set (with
viands) that there may be for us—for the first
and the last of us—a solemn festival [emphasis
added] and a Sign from Thee...." Allah said: "I
will send it down unto you: But if any of you
after that resisteth faith, I will punish him with
a chastisement such as I have not inflicted on
any one among all the peoples"*
Quran 5:112-115

In various other passages of the Quran, we have
seen that Muhammad sometimes got details from different
biblical stories mingled together. Remember, he was a man
with no formal schooling and what he got regarding Christianity, he got by listening to either Christians or Jews
telling him. For example, in the quranic account of God
clothing Adam and Eve, He clothes them with garments of
many colors. Whereas the Bible says He clothed them with
the skins of animals. Here Muhammad mingled the details
from the story of Joseph with the account of Adam and Eve.

In the above quranic passage there are several elements from different biblical accounts that are intermixed. For example, in John 6:30-31, the Jews were asking God for a miracle such as Moses did: "He gave them bread from heaven to eat." So it is possible that this account got imbedded into the quranic passage. But this is not where we want to go with this.

In the above quote, from Quran 5, the words "a solemn festival" have been italicized. Those are the words that fascinate us. The use of this word "festival" (*eid* in Arabic) could only refer to what we call "the Lord's Supper."

To help our Muslim friend understand what Muhammad may have heard from Christians, we need to have him or her read two passages from the Scriptures that may throw light on this matter. The first one is, "For the bread of God is He who comes down from heaven and gives life to the world" (John 6:33). And, "I am the living bread that came down from heaven" (John 6:51). Here Jesus is clearly stating that He is Life. In Him is life (John 14:6), and outside of Him is death (i.e., "The wages of sin is death," Rom. 6:23).

From the passages in the Gospel of John above, now show your friend what Jesus did the night before He was put on the cross. This is found in Matthew 26:26-29:

> While they were eating, Jesus took bread, gave thanks and broke it, and gave it to His disciples, saying, "Take and eat. This is My body." Then He took the cup, gave thanks and offered it to them saying, "Drink from it, all of you. This is My blood of the covenant, which is poured out for many for the forgiveness of sins. I tell you, I will not drink of this fruit of the vine from now on until that day when I drink it anew with you in My Father's kingdom."

Unless he or she has read the Bible, no Muslim has ever read or heard such astonishing words. Probably at first reading or hearing, there will be no comprehension of what this is really saying.

As you begin to explain the real meaning of Jesus' words above, be sure to remind them that this is *"the solemn festival"* being referred to in the Quran.

This necessarily leads into a discussion of the teaching of the Prophet Ezekiel, "The soul that sins is the one who will die" (Ezek. 18:4b). This is just an echo of what God said in the Book of Moses, "You must not eat from the tree of the knowledge of good and evil, for when you eat of it you shall surely die" (Gen. 2:17).

*"The Solemn Festival"* refers to our celebration of Jesus' death on the cross for our sins and the promise of his return.

You may want to turn to the Apostle Paul's words (1 Cor. 11:23-30), and note especially the words, "Whenever you eat this bread and drink this cup, you proclaim the Lord's death until He comes" (1 Cor.11:26). May the Lord bless you and lead you as you open up this sacred subject with your Muslim friend.

# JESUS AS A SERVANT OF GOD

In the Quran Jesus, among other things, is called a servant of God. We are going to look at the following two quranic passages and then see how we can use the concept to help our Muslim friends understand what the ancient books (the Bible) say about Jesus as servant. In Q. 4:172 and 19:30 (M.H. Shakir translation), we read: "The Messiah does by no means disdain that he should be a servant of God.[1]" "He [Jesus] said: 'Surely I am a servant of God: He has given me the Book [that is, the Gospel] and made me a prophet.'"

As we begin this study with our Muslim friend, we may need to remind him or her that the Quran in 3:50 and 5:46 asserts that Jesus came in His day to confirm what was in the Law of Moses. By extending this principle of confirming the previous Scriptures, He also was to confirm what was in the Psalms of David and the Prophets. Yet there is no mention in the Quran of what He was confirming or how He would fulfill these prophecies in both word and deed.

This is where you come in, my Christian friend. The Bible is so rich in details of what Jesus' servanthood entails. It is your privilege to lead your Muslim friends to see for themselves what was written in the books before Jesus came.

Here, you should have your Bible open to Matthew 5:17, and together read Jesus' own words: "Do not think

---

[1] For purposes of this study, "Allah" has been translated as "God."

that I have come to abolish the Law or the Prophets; I have not come to abolish them but to fulfill them."

Alongside this, read another way in which Jesus expressed His own purpose in coming: "[T]he Son of Man did not come to be served, but to serve, and to give His life as a ransom for many" (Mark 10:45).

In the Law and the Prophets the word "ransom" is used to mean "paying the price to set someone free." As Jesus was about to begin his ministry, another prophet named John (*Yahya* in Arabic) saw Jesus coming to him for baptism and exclaimed: "Look, the Lamb of God who takes away the sin of the world" (John 1:29).

The prophet John the Baptist knew the Law of Moses (dated 1400 B.C.). He knew all about the sacrifices mentioned in it and in the Prophets. He knew about the Day of Atonement. On this day, sacrifices were offered by the high priest to cover or atone for the sins of the people. You may want to read Numbers 29:7-11 describing the sacrifices to be made on this day. Notice the references to the lamb sacrifices. These were called "sin offerings." By them one's sins were symbolically washed away or atoned for. John the Baptist recognized, as a prophet, that Jesus was going to be the sacrificial lamb.

John the Baptist also knew that in the book of one of the great prophets, there was a whole section devoted to this special, sacrificial lamb. With your Muslim friend, now turn to Isaiah (written 700 years before Christ) and read from 52:13 through 53:12. Please call attention to the following statements:

- "His appearance was so disfigured beyond that of any man" (52:14).

- "He was despised and rejected by men" (53:3).

- "He was pierced for our transgressions" (53:5).

- "He was led like a lamb to the slaughter" (53:7).

- "He was assigned a grave with the wicked and with the rich in His death" (53:9).

- "After the suffering of His soul, He will see the light [of life]" (53:11).

- "By His knowledge [Jesus] will justify many, and He will bear their iniquities" (53:11).

The story of Jesus' suffering and crucifixion is written in all four gospels. Together, they form a complete picture. May I suggest the Apostle John's account, (John 19:1 - 20:31). Here you may call attention to the following:

- Jesus was flogged with a leather whip with bits of metal in it to cut the flesh.

- A crown of thorns was pressed down on His head and soldiers struck Him.

- The Roman governor handed Him over to be crucified.

- After hours of suffering, Jesus cried out, "It is finished," and then He died.

- The soldiers thrust a spear into Jesus' side to make sure He was dead.

- Jesus was buried in a rich man's tomb.

- On the third day, Jesus rose from the dead.

- Jesus gave the Holy Spirit to His disciples.

- This all happened "that you may believe that Jesus is the Christ, the Son of God, and that by believing you may have life through His name" (John 20:31).

All of the above are illustrations of what was implied in the words that Jesus would be a servant of God. He came to fulfill the will of God as a servant. And what was God's will? It is so well expressed in this famous verse, "For God so loved the world that He gave His one and only Son, that whoever believes in Him shall not perish but have eternal life" (John 3:16). It's all about God's love for lost sinners and His rescue plan to save (ransom) all who would believe through Jesus the Messiah.

The Apostle Paul summarized the meaning of all of this so beautifully as follows:

> *[Christ Jesus] who, being in very nature*
> *God, did not count equality with God some-*
> *thing to be grasped, but made Himself nothing,*
> *taking the very nature of a **servant**, being*
> *made in human likeness. And being found in*
> *appearance as a man, He humbled Himself*
> *and became obedient to death—even death on a*
> *cross. Therefore God exalted Him to the highest*
> *place and gave Him the name that is above*
> *every name, that at the name of Jesus every*
> *knee should bow...and every tongue confess*
> *that Jesus Christ is Lord,*
> *to the glory of God the Father.*
> Philippians 2:6-11

# JESUS AS AN EXAMPLE

In so many ways, the Quran provides Christians with a way to fully introduce our Muslim friends to what they refer to as the Ancient Scriptures (the Law of Moses, the Psalms of David, the Prophets and the Gospel) and ultimately to the Jesus they do not know. These carefully chosen verses from the Quran, thus, serve as stepping stones to eternity for those who come to believe in Him. In this light, remember what Jesus said in His great prayer to God the Father on the eve of his crucifixion: "Now this is eternal life: that they may know You, the only true God, and Jesus Christ whom You have sent" (John 17:3).

One of these amazing stepping stones is a passage where Jesus is called both a servant and an example. Let's look at Quran 43:59: "He [Jesus] was no more than a servant: We granted our favor to Him, and we made him an example to the Children of Israel."

The previous chapter was a study on Jesus as "servant." We noted that He came to serve and to give His life as a ransom for many. In this present study, please invite your Muslim friend to look with you into the Gospel to see how God sent Jesus to be an example.

As we begin, turn with your Muslim friend to a very famous and well-loved passage where Jesus Himself invites us to come and learn from Him, Matthew 11:28-30, "Come to Me, all you who are weary and burdened, and I will give you rest. Take My yoke upon you and learn from Me, for I am gentle and humble in heart, and you will find rest for your souls. For My yoke is easy and My burden is light."

At this point, you will have to do a bit of explaining. What are our burdens? Put briefly, our burden is our sin and consequent penalty of death and judgment to follow.

Sin is sin because it is revealed as such by the Law of God. You may want to show your Muslim friend 2 Corinthians 3:6, where it says, "[T]he letter [i.e., the Law] kills, but the Spirit gives life."

The reason the law kills is that it convicts when we disobey. At the end of time comes the judgment. Thus, sin becomes our burden and leaves us fearing death and judgment. Jesus came to take the burden of all this away.

As we have already learned, Jesus came as the Lamb of God, to take the sins of the whole world into Himself as a once-and-for-all sacrifice, and die in our place, thereby satisfying the demands of the death penalty that was on us all. If we believe in Him and the Father who sent Him, that person "...has eternal life and will not be condemned; he has crossed over [spiritually] from death to life" (John 5:24b).

Not only does Jesus invite us to come and learn all of this from Him, but He became an example for us. In this world, suffering is universal. Injustices abound in every land. Wars begin over these grievances. But Jesus' way is different. He said to the Roman ruler of His day, "My kingdom is not of this world. If it were, My servants would fight to prevent My arrest by the Jews. But now My kingdom is from another place" (John 18:36). He chose the way of suffering and, consequently, became an example for us. You must read the verse above with your Muslim friend and then turn to 1 Peter 2:21, where we read, "To this you were called, because Christ suffered for you, leaving you an example, that you should follow in His steps."

Explain to your Muslim friend that it was Jesus' extraordinary love that characterized His whole life and ministry. Just as at the end of His life He gave Himself as a sacrifice for us all, so in His days before the crucifixion, He exhibited His love in a truly astonishing way. By now, you should have your Bible open to John 13:1-17, and read it together. Jesus knew that His time to leave this world was drawing near. Before He died, He who allowed Himself to be called "Teacher" and "Lord" wanted to show His disciples the full extent of His love. To their amazement, He began to wash the feet of each one of His disciples. When He was through, this is what He said to them: "Now that I, your Lord and Teacher, have washed your feet, you also should wash one another's feet. I have set you an example that you should do as I have done for you" (John 13:14-15).

What an example Christ has been! Through these selections from the *Injil*, Jesus tells us that He is "gentle and humble in heart." He humbled Himself to wash His disciples' feet. In his love and humility, He gave Himself as a sacrificial Lamb for the sins of the whole world. He is an incredible example—like no other! And we are invited to look to Him now. Please read these words of Hebrews 12:2-3 with your Muslim friend:

> *Let us fix our eyes on Jesus, the author and perfecter of our faith, who for the joy set before Him endured the cross, scorning its shame, and sat down at the right hand of the throne of God. Consider Him who endured such opposition from sinful men, so that you will not grow weary and lose heart.*

# JESUS AS THE SIMILITUDE OF ADAM

In both the Quran and the Bible, there is only one reference in each book linking Jesus' name with that of Adam. The quranic reference, Q. 3:59, is actually quite short, with no further comment. It reads, "The similitude of Jesus before God is that of Adam; He created him from dust, then said to him, 'Be': and he was." The implication from this quranic reference is that Jesus was created and, therefore, is not eternal. Part of the reference to Adam in the Quran refers back to the original creation account in the first book of the Bible, namely, Genesis 2:7, "[T]he Lord God formed the man ["Adam," in Hebrew] from the dust of the ground and breathed into his nostrils the breath of life, and the man became a living being."

It is when we turn to the passage in the Bible which links Jesus' name with Adam's that we notice new and startling material that may be of interest to your Muslim friend. Have your friend look with you at the following passage in 1 Corinthians 15:42-49. This is in the context of a discussion on the resurrection:

> So it will be with the resurrection of the dead. The [human] body that is sown is perishable, it is raised imperishable. It is sown in dishonor [referring to the decay following death], it is raised in glory; it is sown in weakness, it is raised in power. It is sown a natural body, it is raised a spiritual body.
>
> If there is a natural body, there is also a spiritual body. So it is written: "The first man Adam became

a living being"; the last Adam, a life-giving spirit.... The first man [Adam] was of the dust of the earth, the second man [Jesus] from heaven. As was the earthly man [Adam], so are those who are of the earth; and is the man from heaven [Jesus], so also are those who are of heaven. And just as we have borne the likeness of the earthly man [Adam], so shall we bear the likeness of the man from heaven [Jesus].

Of course, no Muslim has even a hint of an idea that Jesus came from heaven. He or she has been told many times that Jesus was just a man of the earth, like the first Adam. So the above passage from the Bible is going to be contrary to all the Muslim preconceived ideas. In response to the above passage, your Muslim friend may blurt out that the Bible has been changed. Please remind your friend that the Quran confirms the previous Scriptures (Q. 10:37), and that there can be no change in the Word of God (Q. 6:34), and if the Muslim wants further understanding on an issue, he or she is to consult with those who had these ancient books before the Quran came (Q. 10:94). Also, you may want to point your friend to the material in the Introduction on the authenticity of the Bible as we have it today.

If your friend is willing to continue with you, you may want to refer to other passages, which speak of Jesus coming down from heaven to do God's will. Please remind your friend that God is a spirit, and therefore does not have a physical body such as we have. Remind your friend that God has chosen to eternally express Himself as the Word and that this Word became flesh and dwelt among us (John 1:14). Furthermore, in order to express Himself to us in the most understandable form possible, God the Father sent Jesus as the express image of Himself (Hebrews 1:3), but as a man – a perfect man. Jesus, in His own words, said such things as:

- "I have come down from heaven not to do My will but to do the will of Him who sent Me" (John 6:38).

- "I am the living bread that came down from heaven" (John 6:51).

- "I am not here on My own, but He who sent Me is true. You do not know Him, but I know Him because I am from Him and He sent Me" (John 7:28b-29).

- "[Y]ou are from below [that is, of the earth]; I am from above [that is, from heaven]. You are of this world; I am not of this world" (John 8:23).

- "[I]f God were your father, you would love Me, for I came from God and now am here. I have not come on My own; but He sent Me" (John 8:42).

- "I came from the Father [that is, God] and entered the world; now I am leaving the world and going back to the Father" [through His death, resurrection and ascension] (John 16:28).

- "Now this is eternal life: that they may know You, the only true God, and Jesus Christ, whom You have sent" (John 17:3).

- "Father, I want those You have given Me to be with Me where I am, and to see My glory, the glory You have given Me because You loved Me before the creation of the world" (John 17:24).

As you sit with your Muslim friend, you may want to go on to explain the following, perhaps with words like this:

All of us, in our current state, are like the first Adam. We too, like him, will return to dust, unless God gives us eternal life. The amazing thing is that God wants us to be saved; He wants to give us eternal life in a heavenly state. To do this, He sent Jesus to us to deal with our problems. Jesus in His lifetime solved our sin problem by taking our sins into His own body and dying on the cross for us (2 Cor. 5:21). He overcame death by rising from the dead. And He defeated Satan by never sinning and fulfilling all the demands of the Law of God for all of us who believe.

So, just as in the first Adam, we all came under the sentence of death, now, in the last Adam [Jesus], by virtue of believing in Him, we become bonded with Him in His great victory over death, and we shall bear His holy image – the nature and character of the One the Father sent to save us. In this sense, then, the last Adam [Jesus] is a life-giving Spirit, giving us eternal life.

Tell your Muslim friend that to receive this eternal life, it is necessary to believe in Jesus for who He *really* is. Here are Jesus' own words:

*[W]hoever hears My word and believes Him who sent Me has eternal life and will not be condemned; he has crossed over from death to life.*
John 5:24

# JESUS AS THE MESSIAH

One more time, please turn with your Muslim friend to this oft-quoted verse that says so much about Jesus, Quran 3:45: "Behold! The angels said: 'O Mary! God giveth thee glad tidings of a Word from Him; his name will be Christ Jesus, the son of Mary, held in honor in this world and in the hereafter and of (the company of) those nearest to God.'"

The Hebrew word "*Meshiach*" means "the Anointed One." In the Greek language, the word for "the Anointed One" is "*Xristo's.*" or "Christ." It is interesting to note that in the Quran, the Arabic word "*Al-Masih*" is used eleven times and is always brought over into English as "Christ" by the translator, Abdullah Yusuf Ali. This translator was well educated and knew the meaning of this word. But the majority of Muslims do not.

This is where you come in, Christian friend. It will be your privilege to explain this.

In this study, if your Muslim friend knows the Quran, he or she will know the passages where it says that Christ was no more than an apostle (Q. 4:171), that Christ was not God (Q. 5:17), and that the Christians[1] called Jesus "the Son of God." In this study, we do not want you to get entangled in a controversy with your Muslim friend. Accordingly, we are suggesting you open up the subject something like this:

---

[1] In Arabic, the Nazaris, obviously is derived from the word "Nazareth," the town where Jesus grew up.

"Dear friend, I was fascinated to read in your holy book that Jesus is mentioned so many times and that he is called 'Christ,' which is the Greek translation of the original Hebrew word '*Meshiach*.' And I have heard that in the Quran, the word is '*Al-Masih*.' But nowhere in the Quran does it give the meaning of this word. It actually means 'the Anointed One.' I was wondering if you would like to see the fascinating ways in which this word occurs in the *Injil*? If you are interested, let's turn to three or four passages.

"First of all, when an angel of the Lord announced the birth of Jesus [*Isa*] to the shepherds on the hills outside of Bethlehem[2], he said, 'Do not be afraid. I bring you good news of great joy that will be for all the people. Today in the town of David [Bethlehem] a Savior has been born to you; He is Christ [*Al-Masih*] the Lord,' (Luke 2:10-11). Here we see that Christ, the Anointed One [*Al-Masih*] is called 'Savior' and 'Lord.'"

Next, you may want to lead your friend to the story of an early Apostle of Jesus, Philip by name, who introduced his friend, Nathanael, to Jesus. Read together John 1:43-51. Call attention to Jesus' ability to read a person's character and to know what Nathanael was thinking when he was out of sight under a fig tree. Nathanael's response was truly amazing. He exclaimed, "Rabbi" [Teacher], You are the Son of God; You are the King of Israel." Here, the expression "Son of God" implies Jesus was to be a king.

Later in His ministry, Jesus asked His disciples who they thought He was (Matt. 16:15). Consider how, by this

---

[2] A town in the West Bank today.

time, the disciples had seen many miracles, including these that are listed in the first fifteen chapters of the book of Matthew:

- Healing every known sickness.

- Delivering people from demons.

- Feeding 5,000 men plus women and children from five loaves and two fish.

- Feeding 4,000 people from seven loaves and a few small fish.

- Giving authority and power to His disciples to preach the Kingdom of God, heal the sick, cast out demons and raise the dead.

The disciples also heard all of His great teaching. In light of all the above, the Apostle Peter, in response to Jesus' question, replied, "You are the Christ, the Son of the living God" (Matt. 16:16). Instead of rebuking Peter for calling Him "the Son of the living God," Jesus called Peter "blessed" and said that the Father in heaven had revealed this to him (Matt. 16:17).

In another study we examine the story of Jesus' healing of the man born blind. Jesus allowed that man with restored vision to call Him "Lord" and to worship Him (John 9:38). In the story of raising Lazarus from the dead, we read what Martha said to Jesus: "I believe that You are the Christ [the Anointed One], the Son of God, who was to come into the world" (John 11:27).

At the crucifixion of Jesus, when darkness covered the earth, when the veil of the temple was torn from the top to the bottom, when the earth shook and rocks split, the Roman soldier who was on duty there, said, "Surely He was the Son of God" (Matthew 27:54).

After He rose from the dead, He walked with two of His disciples and opened their understanding to all the prophecies that were fulfilled by His death and resurrection and He said (Luke 24:46-47), "'This is what is written: The Christ [the Anointed One, *Al-Masih*] will suffer and rise from the dead on the third day, and repentance and forgiveness of sins will be preached in His name to all nations, beginning at Jerusalem.'"

Jesus, the Christ, the Anointed One, truly is as all of the above testified, the Lord, the Son of God, and the Savior of the world.

# JESUS' ETERNAL ROLES

# JESUS AS CREATOR

Dear Christian friend, as you seek to relate to your Muslim friend or neighbor, remember he or she already has a preconceived idea, learned from the Quran, that Jesus was only a prophet for His day. Muslims believe He was only a mortal man, a very special one to be sure, but not divine.

Dear Muslim friend, as you read this study, remember that it is said in the Quran that it was given to confirm the Scriptures that came before it: "To Thee we sent the Scripture in truth, confirming the scripture which came before it..." (Q. 5:48). We invite you to stay with us as we go back to those treasured books for fuller details.

As we take up this subject of Jesus as Creator, we will first look at the quranic testimony to this, and then to ancient Scriptures that the Quran purports to confirm.

In Quran 3:49, the following words are attributed to Jesus: "...I make for you out of clay, as it were, the figure of a bird, and breathe into it, and it becomes a bird..." In Quran 5:110, supposedly God is speaking to Jesus when he says: "And behold! Thou makest out of clay, as it were, the figure of a bird, by My leave, and thou breathest into it, and it becometh a bird..."

These are strange words for those of us who have a much fuller description of Christ's activities in the New Testament. But we must not be surprised when we consider the kind of stories that were circulating in Muhammad's environment (570-632 A.D.). There is a body of literature

99

called the "Apocryphal Gospels" in which we find a quote attributed to the "Gospel of Thomas," a fifth- or sixth-century book written in the Syriac language. This so-called gospel, of course, was never a part of the inspired scriptures that we call the New Testament.

Here is the quote that Muhammad would have heard in his day: "And having made soft clay, he fashioned thereof twelve sparrows...Jesus clapped his hands and cried out to the sparrows and said to them: 'Go!' And the sparrows took their flight and went away chirping." (James, 1924, p. 49.) From this kind of background information, we can see that Muhammad was being true to the information he had at hand, considering that the Bible had not been translated into Arabic until more than a hundred years after Muhammad died.

In leading our Muslim friend to the Ancient Books [the Bible], we already have studied one "stepping stone" where Jesus is called the "Word of God" in both the Quran (Q. 3:45: Q. 4:171) and the Bible (John 1:1-3, 14). Particularly, we want to review the words in John 1:3, "Through Him [Jesus, the Word of God] all things were made; without Him nothing was made that has been made."

Now if Jesus were just a mere man, this would not be possible. But in the same passage, John 1:1, we read: "In the beginning was the Word, and the Word was with God, and the Word was God." Jesus was more than a mere man. He claimed to be one with God the Father (John 10:30). He said that he who had seen Him had seen God the Father (John 14:9) and that He was in the Father and the Father was in Him (John 10:38).

In His own days of ministry on earth, we read of Jesus' creative power. Invite your Muslim friend to look with you at John 2:1-11, where Jesus turned water into wine at the wedding party. Or turn to John 6:1-15, where He multiplied five small barley loaves and two small fish into enough food to feed five thousand people with twelve baskets of food left over.

It is when we get to the other New Testament writers that we read of the full extent of Jesus' deity as Creator. In the letter to the church at Colosse, by the inspiration of the Holy Spirit, Paul wrote that: "For by Him [Jesus] all things were created: things in heaven and on earth, visible and invisible, whether thrones or powers or rulers or authorities; all things were created by Him and for Him" (Colossians 1:16). This doesn't leave anything out, does it?

Even Solomon understood this when he wrote of the Christ to come (wisdom personified), quoting Christ's claims: "I was appointed from eternity, from the beginning, before the world began...I was the craftsman at His [God the Father's] side..." (Proverbs 8:23, 30).

Finally, in the book of Hebrews, we read the following:

> In the past God spoke to our forefathers through the prophets at many times and in various ways, but in these last days He has spoken to us by His Son, whom He [God the Father] appointed heir of all things, and through whom He made the universe. The Son is the radiance of God's glory and the exact representation of His being, sustaining all things by His powerful word (Heb. 1:1-3a).

We thank God that this tiny reference to Jesus' creativity was found in the Quran so that we could use it to move us back to the ancient Scriptures and find the fullest possible description of who Jesus really is as the Creator, the agency of God's will in bringing all things into being by His powerful word. He is the one who in the last book of the Bible says:

*"I am making everything new."*
Revelation 21:5

# JESUS AS NEAREST TO GOD

What a joy to take these quranic references to Jesus and use them as stepping stones back into the richness of the Ancient Scriptures. Jesus from the Quran to the Bible is a pathway of delight.

We have looked at Quran 3:45 several times already. It is filled with rich references to many aspects of Jesus' entrance into the world. In this study, we are going to look at the phrase "Jesus...of those nearest to God." Here is the complete verse, "Behold! The angels said: 'O Mary! God giveth thee glad tidings of a Word from Him; his name will be Christ Jesus, the son of Mary, held in honor in this world and the Hereafter and *of those nearest to God*'" (emphasis added).

What does this mean "of those nearest to God"? Fortunately, the Quran itself gives us a way to find out. The clue is found in Quran 5:68, "O People of the Book! Ye have no ground to stand upon unless ye stand fast by the Torah, the Gospel, and all the revelation that has come to you from your Lord."

To gain light on what the Quran might be alluding to, we have the pleasure of consulting biblical material. For us, this comes in two eras: the days of Jesus' actual ministry on earth, and then after His ascension to heaven, the words He gave to the Apostle John in the last book of the Bible called "Revelation."

Nothing is more revealing than the intimacy of one's prayer life. What would a man pray the same night that he is going to be arrested and tortured in preparation for his execution on a cross the next day? We have it! Jesus' great prayer is found in the Gospel written by the Apostle John. All of chapter 17 is Jesus' prayer. Invite your Muslim friend to sit with you as you read this out loud or have him or her do it. Having done that, we suggest you go back and highlight the following excerpts from this prayer, "I have brought You glory on earth by completing the work You gave Me to do. And now, Father, glorify Me in Your presence with the glory I had with You before the world began" (John 17:4-5). "My prayer is not for them [His disciples] alone. I pray also for those who will believe in Me through their message, that all of them may be one, Father, just as You are in Me and I am in You" (John 17:20-21a).

Notice two things in the above: 1) Jesus was with the Father before the world began, and, 2) Jesus and the Father are one—the Father is in Jesus and Jesus is in the Father.

This is as close as you can get. This is an echo of what Jesus said earlier in His ministry, "I and the Father are one" (John 10:30). Furthermore:

> Anyone who has seen Me has seen the Father. How can you say, 'Show us the Father'? Don't you believe that I am in the Father, and that the Father is in Me? The words I say to you are not just My own. Rather, it is the Father, living in Me, who is doing His work. Believe me when I say that I am in the Father and the Father is in Me; or at least believe on the evidence of the miracles themselves. John 14:9b-11

Nothing could be clearer than these statements. They dramatically reinforce the biblical teaching from start to finish that God is one. Not only is Jesus among those nearest to God, as the Quran affirms, but He is intrinsically the expression of God in human form. These words from the opening chapter of John's gospel spell it out so clearly, "No one has ever seen God, but God the One and Only, who is at the Father's side, has made Him known" (John 1:18).

To quote from another place in the Scriptures, Hebrews 1:2-3a, we read the following: "[I]n these last days He has spoken to us by His Son, whom He appointed heir of all things, and through whom He made the universe. The Son is the radiance of God's glory and the exact representation of His being."

The intimacy between God the Father and God the Son is more than "near." They are one! As difficult as this is to understand, it is nevertheless very important. Jesus knew who and what He was. The Father sent Him as His exact representation into the world. This is why Jesus said in John 5:23b, "He who does not honor the Son does not honor the Father who sent Him."

In symbolic language in the last book of the Bible we see just how near Jesus is to God (Rev. 5:13):

*Then I heard every creature in heaven and on earth...*
*singing: 'To Him who sits on the throne and to the Lamb [in*
the center of the throne] *be praise and honor and glory and*
*power for ever and ever!'*

# JESUS AS THE WORD OF GOD

As we look to this subject concerning Jesus as the Word of God, there are certain things to keep in mind. The first is that Muslims have been taught a different view of Jesus Christ than what we have in the Bible. This may lead the Muslim to be argumentative.

Your attitude, your demeanor initially may be more important than what you say. How do you come across to your Muslim friend? In the following passage, where the Apostle Paul was counseling his young disciple, Timothy, we read the following advice:

Don't have anything to do with foolish and stupid arguments, because you know they produce quarrels. And the Lord's servant *must not quarrel*; instead, he must *be kind* to everyone, *able to teach, not resentful.* Those who oppose him he must *gently* instruct, in the hope that God will grant them repentance leading them to a knowledge of the truth, and that they will come to their senses and escape from the trap of the devil, who has taken them captive to do his will (emphasis added) (2 Tim. 2:23-26).

There is both a "truth" dimension to what we do as well as a "spiritual" one. Your friend has been in the grip of a powerful deception. So as you reason with him or her, you must also be in prayer that God, by His Spirit, will remove the veil from their minds and give your friend the grace to receive what you are about to share. Also, please note these qualities in your conduct: *Don't quarrel. Be kind.*

107

*Be able to teach [prepare yourself]. Don't be resentful. And above all, be gentle.*

Now, let's have a look at our key verses in the Quran. The first reference is found in the passage where Muhammad is retelling the story of the angel Gabriel appearing to Mary announcing the birth of Jesus; the second reference is where God is supposedly warning Christians to commit no excesses in their religion: "O Mary! Allah [God] giveth thee glad tidings of a Word from Him: his name will be Christ Jesus, the son of Mary..." (Quran 3:45). "Christ Jesus the son of Mary was a Messenger of God and His Word,..." (Quran 4:171).

Please ignore any discussion, if you can, on Muhammad's emphasis on Jesus being the son of Mary. This was Muhammad's favorite expression, borrowed from a sect of Christians that referred to Jesus this way. Don't get into a discussion of Jesus being the Son of God.

We must dwell only on the phrases *"a Word from Him,"* and *"His Word."* In the centuries after Muhammad died, Muslim theologians debated the issue of whether the Word of God was created or uncreated. By the time of the most famous Muslim commentator, al-Bidawi, who died in 1291 A.D., the Muslim scholars decided that the Word of God was uncreated, that is, eternal. Remember this, because it leads into our use of our own inspired Scriptures.

Your approach could go something like this:

*Mahboob* [a Muslim name meaning "beloved"], I have read in your Quran that Jesus is called 'a Word from God,' and 'His [that is, God's] Word.' But in the Quran, I have found no further explanation of what the Word of God [Jesus] does or is. So I turned to the

STEPPING STONES TO ETERNITY

ancient Scriptures, which the Quran recommends we do when we want further enlightenment on a subject (Q. 10:94), and I found an amazing passage that throws tremendous light on this subject.

Here you, the Christian friend, should have your Bible open to John chapter one. You might say something like, "Would you like to look at this with me?" Or, "Here, read this." What you will read is the following:

In the beginning was the Word, and the Word was with God, and the Word was God. He [Jesus, the Word] was with God in the beginning. Through Him [Jesus, the Word] all things were made; and without Him [Jesus, the Word] nothing was made that has been made. In Him [Jesus, the Word] was life, and that life was the light of men (John 1:1-4).

Then skip ahead to verse 14 and have your friend read it too: "The Word [Jesus] became flesh and made His dwelling among us. We have seen His glory, the glory of the One and Only, who came from the Father, full of grace and truth" (John 1:14).

Remember, Muslims believe that God only has to speak and say, "Be!" and things come into existence (Q. 3:47). You must find a way to explain that Jesus is that expression of God, the Word of God. You may want to use Hebrews 1:2-3 here. It reinforces the above, explaining that Jesus is the radiance of God's glory and the exact representation of His being. Thus, Jesus is the expression of God Himself, through whom He does all things.

Of course, these ideas are new and even explosive in the mind of your Muslim friend. Be very patient as he or she tries to break out of the prison-house of deception and tries to comprehend these revolutionary and breath-taking ideas about Jesus. Be praying that God will open the eyes of their understanding as to who Jesus really is. If they can comprehend this, they have also accepted the idea that Jesus is the Son of God, the most difficult thing for a Muslim to accept. Pray that God will lead you to a Muslim and try this approach with him or her. May God open a door for your witness.

# JESUS AS A MERCY FROM GOD

In the Quran, there is only one verse that refers to Jesus as a "mercy" from God. The reference, Quran 19:21, occurs when an unnamed angel appears to the Virgin Mary in the form of a man announcing the birth of her son. She asks how this may be and these words are part of the answer: "The Lord saith, 'That is easy for Me: and (We wish) to appoint him as a sign unto men and a mercy from Us.'"

Before attempting this study, the worker should read the whole of the first chapter of the Gospel of Luke. It is here that we find both Mary and Zechariah referring to Jesus' birth as a mercy from God.

While visiting her cousin, Elizabeth, who is the mother of John the Baptist, Elizabeth pronounced a great blessing on Mary. Mary in response replied with a beautiful song of praise. In this song, she expresses these words from Luke 1:50, 54-55: "His *mercy* extends to those who fear Him, from generation to generation.... He has helped his servant Israel, remembering to be *merciful* to Abraham and his descendants forever, even as He said to our fathers" (emphasis added).

Later, after the birth of John the Baptist, his father Zechariah bursts into a song of praise, recorded in Luke 1:68-79. Please have your Muslim friend read this with you. It includes such phrases as:

Praise be to the Lord...He has come and has *redeemed* His people. He has raised up a horn [a symbol of strength] of *salvation* for us...to show *mercy* to our fathers and to remember...the oath He swore to our father Abraham...And you, my child [John the Baptist] will be called a prophet of the Most High; for you will go on before the Lord [Jesus] to prepare the way for Him, to give His people the knowledge of *salvation* through *the forgiveness of their sins*, because of *the tender mercy* of our God...to shine on those living in darkness and *in the shadow of death*, to guide our feet into *the path of peace* (emphasis added).

Please notice the highly significant words that explain the nature of this mercy that God is going to show through Jesus: "redeemed," "salvation" (mentioned twice), "the forgiveness of sins," and "the path of peace." To understand why these words are so significant, we must keep in mind certain universal truths about the awful circumstances concerning human life today. First of all, death is the one great universal fact about man. It began with our first mother and father, Adam and Eve. In the biblical account, found in Genesis 2:8-3:19 (and it would be good to read this now), we discover that first the woman, and then the man, disobeyed God in eating fruit from the forbidden tree of the knowledge of good and evil. The Lord had said, "If you eat from this tree you will die" (Gen. 2:17). From this first act of disobedience, which the Bible calls "sin," death was introduced into the world.

The second great universal truth is that all men and women sin. In one way or another, we all come short of the standard that the Lord has set for us to follow. The universality of sin and death are referred to in the following biblical passages. Have your Muslim friend read these passages carefully and thoughtfully:

- "All have sinned and fall short of the glory of God" (Romans 3:23).

- "The wages of sin is death..." (Rom. 6:23).

- "Therefore, just as sin entered the world through one man, and death through sin, and in this way death came to all men, because all sinned" (Rom. 5:12).

- "Man is destined to die once, and after that to face judgment" (Heb. 9:27).

As a result of the universality of death and the sin, all men are in search of mercy. All men long to be saved from death and the horror of judgment to follow. The Quran calls Jesus "a mercy from God." But it does not explain how Jesus is that mercy. We have to turn back to the earlier Scriptures to find out in what way Jesus is that mercy.

If God were to show mercy to us, what would it look like? It would be a mercy to save us from the consequence of our sin, to actually forgive our sins, and even to save us from the desire to go on sinning. Such a mercy would remove from us the sentence of death and open the door to eternal life in the presence of a loving God, who calls Himself "our Father," and who would call us "His children." Mercy would deliver us from the dark fear of judgment.

Was Jesus sent as a mercy to us to accomplish the things above? Yes, that is why God the Father sent Him. There are two passages in the first epistle (letter) of Peter that help explain this, 1 Peter 2:24, and 1 Peter 3:18a. Let's read them: "He Himself [Jesus] bore our sins in His body on the tree [the cross], so that we might die to sins and live for righteousness; by His wounds you have been healed." "For Christ died for sins once for all, the righteous for the unrighteous, to bring you to God."

In another study we read Jesus' own words, "...to

give His life as a ransom for many" (Matt. 20:28). The word "ransom" means to pay the price for someone to go free. In this case, the price was the blood of the Lord Jesus shed on the cross. Another word for this is "redeem," which means to pay the price to recover someone. This is what Zechariah was singing about, "Praise be to the Lord...because He has come and redeemed his people," (Luke 1:68).

"Jesus Christ [*Isa Al-Masih*] gave Himself for us to redeem us from all wickedness and to purify for Himself a people that are His very own, eager to do what is good" (Titus 2:13b-14).

What must we do to be "ransomed" or "redeemed," to receive the mercy of God? Believe on the Lord Jesus Christ.

# JESUS AS THE RIGHTEOUS ONE

*And he [Jesus] shall be (of the company) of the righteous.*
Quran 3:46b

*I am only a messenger from thy Lord, (to announce)
to thee [Mary] the gift of a pure son [Jesus].*
Quran 19:19

Here we have two stepping stones that lead us to Jesus and beyond into eternity.

One of the remarkable things that you will find in the Muslim world is the idea that Jesus was sinless. It reminds us of Jesus' words in John 8:46, "Can any of you prove me guilty of sin?

None could, of course. No other person on this earth has been able to make such a claim—to be utterly without sin. Jesus was the embodiment of pure righteousness.

As you sit with your Muslim friend to think about these things together, you may want to explore all the dimensions of Jesus' righteousness:

- He was in a right relationship to God the Father throughout His entire life.

- He carried out God's beautiful plan to save us from sin, judgment and death.

- He was in a right relationship to all human beings.

    In 1 Timothy 2:3-4, we read, "...God our Savior...

wants all men to be saved and to come to the knowledge of the truth." This was a fulfillment of a prophecy made six hundred years earlier by the prophet Jeremiah (Jer. 31:3): "...I have loved you with an everlasting love; I have drawn you with loving-kindness."

- He was in a right relationship with His enemies: From the cross, He prayed for their forgiveness (Luke 23:34), "Father, forgive them, for they do not know what they are doing."

- And He was in a right relationship with regard to Satan, the enemy of us all.

When it was time for Him to go to the cross, this is what Jesus said: "I will not speak with you much longer, for the prince of this world [Satan] is coming. He has no hold on Me, but the world must learn that I love the Father and that I do exactly what My Father has commanded Me" (John 14:30-31).

Long ago, through the prophet David, this prophecy was given in Psalm 45:6-7: "Your throne, O God, will last for ever and ever; a scepter of justice will be the scepter of your kingdom. You love righteousness and hate wickedness; therefore God, your God, has set You above Your companions by anointing You with the oil of joy."

As strange as it may seem, this prophecy is about David's most famous descendant, the Lord Jesus Christ. We know this because under the inspiration of the Holy Spirit, the writer of the book of Hebrews quotes this very prophecy and applies it to the Son of God. Please look at this in Hebrews 1:8-10, where Psalm 45:6-7, is quoted, "But about the Son [Jesus, Son of God] He says, 'Your throne, O God, will last forever and ever...You have loved righteousness and hated wickedness; therefore God, Your God, has set You above Your companions by anointing You with the oil of joy."

What are the implications of this for us today? Well, the answer is very profound. At his baptism, Jesus explained to His cousin, the prophet John the Baptist (*Yahya* in Arabic), who protested that Jesus should baptize him and not the other way around, "Let it be so now; it is proper for us to do this to fulfill all righteousness." (Matt. 3:15)

What did Jesus mean by this? On the cross, just before He died, Jesus cried out, "It is finished!" (John 19:30). What was finished? All righteousness. Sin had been atoned for by the blood of Jesus. Man's separation from God had been overcome and the possibility for intimacy with God restored.

Later, in a letter to the churches, the Apostle John wrote (1 John 2:2), "He is the atoning sacrifice for our sins, and not only for ours but also for the sins of the whole world." God required a perfect, sinless sacrifice. Only Jesus, the Righteous One, was qualified to make that sacrifice.

The Apostle Peter, by the inspiration of the Holy Spirit, understood this and wrote in 1 Peter 3:18, "...Christ died for sins once for all, the righteous for the unrighteous, *to bring you to God*" (emphasis added).

There it is, the connection between Jesus Christ, the Righteous one, and your home with God for all eternity!

# A FINAL WORD

As we work with our Muslim friends, we would do well to remember the teaching of Jesus in the parable of the sower and the four kinds of soil (Matthew 13:1-9, 18-23).

I believe Jesus was evaluating His own ministry and preparing His disciples for what to expect as they sowed the gospel seed in the fields of the world.

Let's look at this parable in terms of the picture of human hearts:

1. Some hearts will be as hard and as unreceptive as concrete. The evil one will snatch away the Word from their resistant hearts.

2. There will be some who gladly receive the Word in the beginning but their faith will wither away in the face of persecution.

3. Some will receive the Word, but preoccupation with the concerns of this life and their obsession with riches will gradually choke the Word and it will not bear any fruit in their lives.

4. Finally, there will be those folks whose hearts are good soil for the seed of the Word of God. The seed will take root, grow and bear fruit according to the quality of the soil.

As Jesus was getting ready to depart this world, He was preparing His disciples for the reality of what they would find in their efforts to spread the good news of the Kingdom of God. He was basically saying, "This is the way it is going to be."

Friends, there is great comfort in this. We should not be surprised by the various results of our effort to sow the seed of the Word of God. You are not to be blamed for the decisions that others take in turning away from the Gospel for whatever reason. Yes, we may mourn for them, even as Jesus did over the city of Jerusalem, but our job is to press on and find the "good soil," that is, those with receptive hearts.

In the end, this is Jesus' battle, and He is the one who said, "I will build my Church and the gates of hell will not overcome it" (Matthew 16:18).

# BIBLIOGRAPHICAL REFERENCES

᯾

Badawi, Jamal. *Muhammad in the Bible.* [Publication information unconfirmed, possibly Halifax, NS: Islamic Information Foundation], 1982.

James, M.R. translator. *The Apocryphal Gospels.* Oxford: Clarendon Press, 1986. (p 49)

Khalidi, Tarif, translator. *The Quran: A New Translation.* New York: Viking, 2008 (p. 169)

McCurry, Don. *Healing the Broken Family of Abraham: New Life for Muslims, Second Edition.* Colorado Springs: Ministries to Muslims, 2011

McCurry, Don. *Tales That Teach.* Colorado Springs: Ministries to Muslims, 2009.

Nurbakhsh, Javad. *Jesus in the Eyes of the Sufis.* London: Khanihai-Nimatullahi Publications, 1992.

Parrinder, Geoffrey. *Jesus in the Quran.* Oxford: Oneworld Publications, 2003. (p. 16)

Schwartz, Stephen. *The Other Islam: Sufism and the Road to Global Harmony.* New York: Doubleday Pubs., 2008. (p. 24)

Shakir, M.H., translator. *The Quran.* Elmhurst, NY: Tahrike Tarsal Qur'an, Inc., 1999.

*The Holy Quran: English Translation of the Meanings and Commentary.* Medina: King Fahd Holy Quran Printing Complex, 1985, revision of the A. Yusuf Ali translation." Then please move this entry with a hanging indent to the bottom of the page after "Shakir, M.H...." and move everything else up.

# QURANIC REFERENCES

# BIBLICAL REFERENCES